PRAISE FOR WATER

Sherry has experienced God's g[...]
fruit. She is a woman of deep p[...]
has been her motivation to pur[...]
heart. Sherry has a profound personal experie[...]
and she vividly couples her personal experiences with the
Word of God. Her understanding will be an inspiration and
instruction to many. I recommend this book.

—GABBY MEJIA
pastor and international speaker
Orlando, FL

Sherry invites us to journey with her as she explores the tests
and trials of biblical characters that also challenge us today. An
overcomer herself, Sherry offers clear insights and a scriptural
perspective that applies directly to our lives.

—REV. DAVE AND SUE WELLS
POAC General Superintendent
decorator, author, and speaker

How beautiful is a timely word! *Water in the Desert* is overflowing with the refreshing promises of God, offering hope for
the weary traveler in a dry and barren land. With this study
of Scripture and a look at her own journey through the Sahara, Sherry gives testimony of how streams of living water can
bring not only survival but revival! The artistic touch of her
husband Todd's art creatively compliments the assuring message that God will provide His people with water throughout
the deserts of life.

—REV. NATHAN AND RACHEL ALBRECHT
lead pastors at FGT Family Church
Leamington, ON

The destination is desired. The promises come from a faithful God. *Water in the Desert* is prepared for those who not only have experienced the real challenges of life, but found the treasure of needing God... of discovering the precious reality of dependency in Him! Join author Sherry Stahl as she candidly shares out of her own encounters with this living God! She opens up not only the possibilities of God's faithfulness but also the way past common barricades that could restrict our access to His power and provision. Graciously she points out the pitfalls of the deceptive mirage, leading her fellow travelers on a pathway to true waters of refreshment, healing, and transformation. Break camp, grab your suitcase, and get ready for this shared journey into the abundance of references to the living waters found in the Word!"

—REV. PEGGY KENNEDY
author, international speaker
and founder of Two Silver Trumpets

With deep insights drawn from experience, personal heartache, and recovery, Sherry brings us back to Father God as she offers down-to-earth guidance, help, and solutions to the everyday situations we all face. It's an awesome book that will be a great help to many!

—SUE AUGUSTINE
motivational speaker and author of several books
including *When Your Past is Hurting Your Present*
and contributor to *Chicken Soup for the Soul*

I have known Sherry for more years than I should say! Friends since childhood, I have seen Sherry go through the deserts in her life with tenacity and a faith firmly rooted in the Word of God. It is no wonder that she has written this fantastic, real, and practical devotional. Deserts are inevitable, so this devotional/workbook will be a tool you'll use again and again. Mark and I count it a privilege to know Sherry, to have had her speak to the women as well as the congregation of our church, and to be among the first to read this devotional. She is the real deal!

—Rev. Mark and Andrea Giancola
lead pastors of Maple Community Church
Maple, ON

Sherry's revelation expressed in *Water in the Desert* is reminiscent of Jesus in conversation with the woman at the well in Samaria (John 4). Trying to quench thirst had brought much disillusionment into her life, and so it is for many today. May I commend Sherry's well-outlined study of the only source that will ever satisfy! God created us to drink from the well of living water! Our souls will thirst as if in a desert until they find the parched thirst quenched from that spring!

—Rev. Donna Thorne
director of Teen Challenge Women's Shelter
former director of Women's Ministries, WOD PAOC
Aurora, ON

Sherry's book is a refreshing and practical guide for anyone who has a desire to soak in Scripture. She will guide you through Biblical stories and give you practical applications that will help you work through your desert experiences and find that fresh living water can miraculously flow in the desert!

—Joanne Goodwin
international speaker
www.joannegoodwin.ca

Sherry's first "desert bloom" is a beautiful one! *Water in the Desert* will refresh your soul, revive your heart, and renew your hope. Come. Drink. Believe. Your desert time really can turn into beautiful gardens!

—Kathy Mainse
co-founder of World Embrace
and former co-host of *100 Huntley Street*

Without God's Word I never would have made it through my desert. It truly is living water that infuses strength and hope into our souls, making each step not only possible, but productive! That living water transforms a desert into a precious place—a place you treasure and thank God for. *Water in the Desert* beautifully captures this truth. Drink deeply, my friend, and live!

—SUE KEDDY
author and Women's Connection Director, WOD PAOC

WATER
IN THE DESERT
40 Devotions to Hydrate your Spirit

SHERRY STAHL
ILLUSTRATIONS BY TODD STAHL
2ND EDITION

WATER IN THE DESERT
Copyright © 2015 by Sherry Stahl

Printed in Canada

ISBN: 978-1-4866-0862-1

Word Alive Press
131 Cordite Road, Winnipeg, MB R3W 1S1
www.wordalivepress.ca

MIX
Paper from
responsible sources
FSC® C016245

Library and Archives Canada Cataloguing in Publication

Stahl, Sherry, 1968-, author
        Water in the desert : 40 devotions to hydrate your spirit / Sherry Stahl.

Issued in print and electronic formats.
ISBN 978-1-4866-0862-1 (pbk.).--ISBN 978-1-4866-0863-8 (pdf).--
ISBN 978-1-4866-0864-5 (html).--ISBN 978-1-4866-0865-2 (epub)

        1. Devotional exercises. I. Title.

BV4832.3.S82 2015   242'.2   C2015-900780-1
                                               C2015-900781-X

This book is dedicated to Gramma Pearl.

I have missed you more than I could ever say. Your influence on my life was immeasurable! My love for God's Word, church, and Braeside all came from you! When I start to get weary, I can hear your voice quoting Philippians 4:13:

"I can do all things through Christ who strengthens me" (NKJV).

Thanks for pouring into my life!
I am forever grateful!

CONTENTS

ACKNOWLEDGMENTS

You don't write a book called *Water in the Desert* without having gone through a few deserts of your own! I'm so thankful for the refreshment God brought me during the Sahara times of my life. When I thought my life was over, I found out it was just beginning. His restorative power has transformed my life, so to Him I could not be grateful enough!

God has blessed my life with so many who have made the journey along the desert path one that I enjoy. So many have been there during the wonderful and woeful times in my life.

Todd, I cannot thank God enough for bringing you into my life! Your love has brought me so much healing. Your encouragement has strengthened me. Your wise advice has kept me pursuing God's call... especially when you told me, "God didn't have you go through the desert just to get sand in your shoes!"

For all of you who are too numerous to mention in one page, I thank you! For those who made the journey difficult, I thank you, too! If it weren't for the desert, I wouldn't appreciate the water. God has taken all the hurt out of the painful past and shown me how He is working *all* things together for His good in my life! May God bless you all!

INTRODUCTION

Life is full of deserts. Well, figuratively speaking, that is! There are arguably only one to three actual deserts in my native Canada, but there sure are deserts of life for people all around our country: times when you feel the sun beating down on you, and the heat dries up your water supply. If you're not careful, dehydration can set in. When that happens, you go from being thirsty to becoming parched; your mouth is dry and sticky. A person begins to moan and groan, feeling tired and lacking energy. If dehydration persists, your skin becomes dry and flaky. Left untreated, dehydration will cause your vision to blur. You won't be able to focus, as it causes mental confusion. At some point, you begin to stop sensing thirst and don't care to drink. Your heart will begin to beat rapidly. Eventually you will collapse. It will begin to shut down your organs and body functions. Completely untreated, it can cause death.

Nothing good can come of physical dehydration, but there is something good to come from spiritual dehydration—thirst! The way to recover from physical and spiritual dehydration is the same: rest and rehydration. Thirst quenched by the life-giving water of the Word of God can strengthen you to become stronger than you were before the dehydration.

While facing the Sahara of my life, I began to experience severe signs of dehydration and was soon to collapse. It was in this time that I decided to do something about my situation. I refused to give in and die. I decided to rehydrate! I began to saturate myself in God's Word. It wasn't a quick fix, but it helped immediately.

If you've ever seen those old black-and-white movies where someone is dehydrated in the desert and they wake up when a cup of water is put to their mouth—well, that was me.

At first you're still kind of incoherent, but the more you drink and rest in Him, the more alive you become! God says,

> *I provide water in the desert... to give drink to my people, my chosen, the people I formed for myself that they may proclaim my praise.*
>
> —Isaiah 43:20–21

As I placed myself by the water, God began to provide water in my desert. As I read the story of the Israelites crossing over from the desert into the Promised Land, through the parting of the Jordan River, I began to get excited! I felt God was saying that I, too, was crossing over into the Promised Land. I realized all the things God had been teaching through my time in the desert. I knew He wanted me to write them down so I could share this refreshing with others.

I began searching all the scriptures that speak of water in the desert. To my shock, there were so many! So many that I had to cut many devotions out and set them aside for a second book. It's good to know that we draw from a well that won't run dry!

In this book, there are forty devotions, one per day—or one every few days, if you're going to do the study guide pages. The speed at which you do the devotions is not important. That you get something out of it is! The devotions look at many of the stories of the Israelites in the desert. 1 Corinthians 10:1–13 talks about how the Bible records their history *"as examples and were written down as warnings for us"* (10:11). I want to learn from my mistakes and not keep making them. If I can learn from someone else's mistakes and save myself some pain... even better!

So, join with me as we look through God's Word and find *Water in the Desert!*

Join the community! Sign up on takethe40daychallenge.com for encouragement along the way!

Know someone else who should Take the 40 Day Challenge? Meet the men's counterpart to *Water in the Desert*: *40 Days in the Man Cave* by Todd Stahl! Learn more on page 276.

How to Read this Book

At the beginning of each section, you'll find an introduction called "Swimming in the Deep End." This is a suggested reading list about scriptures that relate to each section. It isn't necessary to read all of these verses to quench your thirst, but it will get you swimming in the deep end of God's Word!

These passages will include the scriptures used in the devotions, but also look at the verses before and after to get a better picture of the whole story and what's going on. The devotions will highlight key points in each of passage.

As you read the passages, try to see people like Hagar, Abraham, Sarah, Moses, and Joshua as real people—because they were! Too often we think of them as Bible "characters," like characters in a play or in a novel. They were real people like you and me. The more you read with this mindset, the more you'll enjoy reading the Bible—and you'll get more out of it. The more you get out of it, the more you'll be able to apply to your life and circumstances.

The forty devotions all follow a familiar format:

WATER: A scripture or group of scriptures that will water your soul.

TREADING WATER: A devotion related to the scripture. This is a time to stay still, keeping a vertical posture, like when treading water, so you can taste how refreshing the water is!

The study guide is located at the back of the book. Each devotion has corresponding workbook pages in the format below that will help you to *dive in deep!*

SOAKING: These are extra scriptures that relate to the topic in the devotion, intended for those days when you have some extra time to soak in the Word! I've included space for you to journal, recording what God reveals to you in His Word.

STARTING TO SWIM: These study guide sections are a call for you to do or focus on something that will help you apply what you've been reading to your life.

Lord...

Wash over me and cleanse me, I pray.

Help me to apply the healing water of Your Word to
   my life.

Saturate my thirsty soul.

Fill me to overflowing.

Let streams of living water pour out of me
   to refresh other thirsty souls and bring You glory!

Amen.

SECTION ONE:
WATER FOR THE WEARY

Swimming in the Deep End: Water for the Weary

The story of Abraham, Sarah, and their servant Hagar is one of the craziest stories told in the Bible, although there are quite a few to choose from. Why would a wife ever come up with a plan to let her husband sleep with her servant and have a baby with the servant because she can't have a baby of her own? Only in the heat of the desert could this possibly make sense. Why would you ever willingly give your husband to another woman? Nothing good could ever come of that.

Genesis 16:2 says, *"And Abram agreed with Sarai's proposal"* (NLT). Well, duh... what man wouldn't? Well, actually, any man with a logical brain wouldn't! It doesn't take rocket science to figure out that this plan could only lead to disaster and heartache for all involved! Sarah, Abraham, Hagar, and their children, Ishmael and Isaac, paid deeply for these bad choices. History has shown that the Middle East—and now the world—continue to pay for the animosity between the descendants of Ishmael and Isaac.

Read the following passages and let your heart ache for Hagar. See the anguish she faced and the hardships she lived through. Be excited as you see how God brings her water in the desert and gives her hope for the future! Believe that God will do the same for you!

Suggested Reading:
Genesis 16:1–16
Genesis 21:9–21
Genesis 25:12

LOSING SIGHT

The Lord has kept me from having children. Go, sleep with my maidservant; perhaps I can build a family through her.

—Genesis 16:2

Sarai and Abraham were so focused on their dream—their promise from God—that they lost sight of right and wrong, the well-being of others, their marriage commitment, and their relationship with God. Their desire for the promise to be fulfilled was no longer about what God wanted and how He desired to bless nations through them; it seemed that what they wanted was to make a name for themselves.

It's too easy to lose your focus from the giver of your dreams to the dream itself. Whenever we take our eyes off the Dreamgiver, we're like Peter walking on the water. Matthew 14 tells of how Jesus came out to the disciples' boat during a storm, walking on water. Peter joins Jesus in walking on the water.

> *But when he saw the wind, he was afraid and, beginning to sink, cried out, "Lord, save me!"*
>
> *Immediately Jesus reached out his hand and caught him. "You of little faith," he said, "why did you doubt?"*
>
> *And when they climbed into the boat, the wind died down. Then those who were in the boat worshiped him, saying, "Truly you are the Son of God."*
>
> —Matthew 14:30–33

Walking on water was impossible for Peter with or without the storm raging. Storms are loud and cause us to listen to what they have to say. The winds can scream lies into our ears, telling us that we're going to drown, we're not going to make it, we don't have what it takes. The wind is partly right, but a liar nonetheless. We don't have what it takes, but if we're smart like Peter, we can call out to someone who has what it takes!

When we choose to call out to Jesus in the time of a storm, to set our focus on His strength and not our weakness, we won't drown. When we devise schemes and situations to *make* God's will happen, we lose sight of what's important. God's promises aren't just for us, but for His glory. God's ultimate desire is relationship with us and the people of our world. It's all about His desire for relationship. It's not about accomplishing; it's not about your reputation or your success.

So don't lose sight. Keep your focus. The dream is about your relationship with Him and how it can bless others.

Do you want to spend more time in the Word? Visit the study guide section at the back of the book to find corresponding "Soaking" and "Starting to Swim" sections for each chapter.

DIVE IN DEEPER ON PAGE 125.

2

DESPERATION CAN LEAD TO CRAZINESS

Now Sarai, Abram's wife, had borne him no children. But she had an Egyptian maidservant named Hagar; so she said to Abram, "The Lord has kept me from having children. Go, sleep with my maidservant; perhaps I can build a family through her."

—Genesis 16:1–2

We can't begin to imagine the public disgrace barrenness was to women in that day and to a family of such great wealth. After many years, the weight of this embarrassment broke Sarai's strength, putting her in such a desperate place that she was willing to do anything to have a baby even if she couldn't give birth to it.

Many women can understand Sarai's pain in not being able to have a child. The longings of a mother's heart for a child can break a woman. It can lead women to endure great pain and expense trying fertility treatments.

Friends of mine twice adopted a baby only to have the mothers come back and take the infants. Those are such crushing blows to the longings of a nurturing heart.

This longing for a child can cause us to cross over into the crazy zone. Newsrooms and newspapers have told the stories of women stealing babies from hospitals to fill their desires for a child. Sometimes life gets so hard that we get crazy ideas—ideas that aren't from God, but come as a result of our desperation. It's even sadder when we're surrounded by people just as crazy as we are who go along with it!

Has God placed people around you who can recognize when your ideas aren't good? Are you listening to them? Well, you may just want to listen and save yourself the heartache of wrong choices and their consequences.

When a person is in the desert and lacking water, they get to the point where their mind hallucinates. They see mirages of oases with plenty of water, but in reality there's only sand. It takes spiritual strength and discernment to know if your idea is God-breathed or desperation delirium!

Proverbs 13:12 says, *"Hope deferred makes the heart sick, but a longing fulfilled is a tree of life."* Waiting for a promise to be fulfilled for a long time makes your heart sick. You want to give up. You want to give in. Don't! Look for God's way out of a situation. Wait for God to fulfill His promise to you... His way, and in His time.

When God's timing for you is fulfilled, it will be a tree of life for you!

Dive in deeper on page 129.

3

THE BLAME GAME

When she [Hagar] knew she was pregnant, she began to despise her mistress. Then Sarai said to Abram, "You are responsible for the wrong I am suffering."
—Genesis 16:4-5

Oh, the blame game—a game that has no winners. Relationships lose when blame is passed on and not taken on. Passing blame tears down friendships, marriages, business partnerships, and family relations. It stirs up resentment.

The knee-jerk reaction to blame is defensiveness. It breaks down any sense of openness between two people and places them in opposition to each other, battling for victory. Even if one "wins," do they really? Even when you've been justifiably hurt, making someone admit their guilt through blame will never bring you closer to them. You may win a battle, but you could lose the war.

Sarai wasn't the first person to blame someone for her unfortunate situation. Adam was. When God confronted Adam about eating from the Tree of Knowledge, a tree God directly told Adam not to eat from, he blamed God and Eve!

The woman you put me here with—she gave me some fruit from the tree, and I ate it.
—Genesis 3:12 (emphasis mine)

Pretty bold, wasn't he? The Bible clearly says that Eve

took some and ate it. She also gave some to her husband, who was with her, and he ate it.
—Genesis 3:6 (emphasis mine)

Eve didn't force Adam to eat it. Adam should have stopped her. He was the one entrusted with the rule, and he was standing right beside her when she took a bite. But don't get all mad at Adam for passing blame, because Eve followed suit. When God confronted her about her disobedience, she said, "The devil made me do it!" (see Genesis 3:13)

Blame broke down Adam and Eve's relationship with God. The Bible tells us that Adam and Eve felt the need to cover up, so they made the first clothing out of fig leaves to hide a part of themselves from God. They knew that they had done wrong. They didn't accept conviction from the Holy Spirit, so it turned into guilt and condemnation.

Blame is a lot of work. It keeps you hiding from your sin and struggling to ensure it stays covered up. It stops you from dealing with your problems and leaves you with guilt. If Adam and Eve had simply accepted their guilt and asked God to forgive them, things would be so much different today. Instead they chose to get rid of their conviction by passing blame. Their disobedience and refusal to accept their guilt caused them to face the consequences of their actions, just like Sarai did.

Blame doesn't bring victory. Blame builds walls that sometimes cannot be broken down. Ask God for His forgiveness and release that forgiveness to others. This will liberate you from the bondage that guilt brings, and propel you to victory!

DIVE IN DEEPER ON PAGE 132.

RUNNING AWAY

I'm running away from my mistress Sarai...

—Genesis 16:8

Who can blame her? I'd want to run away, too, if I were Hagar! It would be depressing to know that you have no rights as a human being. Being used by two selfish rich people to fulfill their own dreams wouldn't be an easy pill to swallow. It sounds harsh, but isn't that the reality of the situation? It was wrong. It was unfair.

When Sarai and Abram were making their plan, they had no consideration for what Hagar thought or what was best for her. In life, at times we don't have any rights—and sometimes when we do, exercising them brings more problems. That's the situation Hagar faced, even though she was the mother of Abram's son.

Jesus understands what it's like to live without rights. Philippians 2:5-11 tells us how Jesus did it:

> *Think of yourselves the way Christ Jesus thought of himself. He had equal status with God but didn't think so much of himself that he had to cling to the advantages of that status no matter what. Not at all. When the time came, he set aside the privileges of deity and took on the status of a slave, became human! Having become human, he stayed human. It was an incredibly humbling process. He didn't claim special privileges. Instead, he lived a selfless, obedient life and then died a selfless, obedient death—and the worst kind of death at that—a crucifixion.*
>
> *Because of that obedience, God lifted him high and honored him far beyond anyone or anything, ever, so that*

*all created beings in heaven and on earth—even those long
ago dead and buried—will bow in worship before this Jesus
Christ, and call out in praise that he is the Master of all, to
the glorious honor of God the Father.*

—Philippians 2:5-11, MSG

Hagar chose to be like Jesus. She humbled herself and
went back as a slave. James 1:3-4 says that

*...the testing of your faith develops perseverance. Persever-
ance must* finish its work *so that you may be mature and
complete, not lacking anything.* (emphasis added)

Instead of running away, run to Him. Make Him your refuge as you allow perseverance to finish its work in you so you
will be mature, complete and not lacking anything! Sounds
like a good tradeoff to me!

DIVE IN DEEPER ON PAGE 135.

— 5 —
POSITION YOURSELF TO MEET WITH GOD

The angel of the Lord found Hagar near a spring in the desert.

—Genesis 16:7

The dehydration people suffer in the desert often causes a host of problems that keep them from finding water. It's a strange phenomenon, but when people are struggling, they often stay away from what they need. People stop reading their Bible, going to church or the gym, going out with their friends, or going to the doctor, dentist, or chiropractor. Their tendency is to close off and keep to themselves.

Left for a long time, isolation shields you—from what can help you. The problems still remain, and usually seem even larger than before. Without getting the help you need, or taking steps to wholeness, you implode. Your thoughts become negative as you focus too much on the problem. This negative thinking turns into a negative attitude—and the negative attitude invades other areas of your thinking. Now you're not just negative about one situation, but most situations that arise. Keeping your negativity bottled up creates a lot of emotional strain that leaves you depleted, dehydrated, and alone.

That's where Hagar was in this story. At the end of her rope, Hagar placed herself near the spring. That was her first important step, but not the one that refreshed her. Hagar had to drink from that spring. As she drank, God refreshed her spirit and gave her strength to go back home and have her baby. Hagar took refuge and refreshment from her God.

If we take refuge in Him—not others, not food, not love, not looks, not relationships, not things—He will be your strength and help you. His Word promises it:

*So do not fear, for I am with you; do not be dismayed, for
I am your God. I will strengthen you and help you; I will
uphold you with my righteous right hand.*

—Isaiah 41:10

Today you have taken the time to place yourself near the
spring by reading this book, and God sees that step. As you
read the verses in the study guide pages, drink deep of the well
that won't run dry and soak in His promises. Place yourself
near other springs, like church, time with encouraging Christian friends, Christian television and DVDs, or whatever it is
that refreshes you. As you position yourself to meet with God,
He will give you water in your desert!

DIVE IN DEEPER ON PAGE 138.

—6—

SOMETIMES GOD CLEANS UP THE MESSES; OTHERS WE FACE

Then Sarai said to Abram, "You are responsible for the wrong I am suffering. I put my servant in your arms, and now that she knows she is pregnant, she despises me. May the Lord judge between you and me..."

Then the angel of the Lord told her, "Go back to your mistress and submit to her." The angel added, "I will so increase your descendants that they will be too numerous to count."

—Genesis 16:5, 9–10

After reading this story, you can see that God would have a lot of judging to do. Both Sarai and Abram did wrong. They both mistreated and blamed each other. It was a vicious cycle of "I'll hurt you, then you'll hurt me, then I'll hurt you back."

This ridiculous plan was Sarai's idea, but Abram knew it wasn't right. He should have been a godly man and said no. He should have comforted his wife's fears and encouraged her by saying that he loved her, children or no children, but that he still believed in God's promise. The craziness would have ended there, and God would have honored his statement of faith.

Instead God honored their choices. As we all know, choices have consequences. A pastor of mine used to say, "We don't break God's laws; God's laws break us." God allowed their choices to be made, and then dealt with the fallout. It seems to me that in this situation, God was a just judge, as Sarai requested. Sarai and Abram were the ones to start this mess, and they had to face the consequences. If they didn't, they would never learn from their mistakes.

Hagar was innocently abused by Sarai and Abram. It wasn't by her choice that she became Abram's mistress or the mother of his child. In the goodness of God, He took this horrible situation and brought good to Hagar. The child Sarai was jealous of, and who was seemingly causing Hagar grief, became the purpose of God for Hagar.

God gave Hagar a promise for her son's life. God promised that out of Ishmael would come an increase of descendants that would be too numerous to count. Ishmael would share in the promise given to his father, Abram. This promise confirmed to Hagar, weak in the desert, that her child wasn't going to die, and that his life had purpose! Hers did, too! If God had such great plans for this child, he would need a mother to train him up for such a great future.

When we are faithful in our desert times, God brings good to us from circumstances that seem to destroy us. He will restore to you what the enemy has stolen away, and give you so much more than you could ever dream!

Dive in deeper on page 141.

7

GOD SEES YOU IN YOUR TIME OF NEED

She gave this name to the Lord who spoke to her: "You are the God who sees me," for she said, "I have now seen the One who sees me."

—Genesis 16:13

How beautiful is the sheer desperation that led to Hagar's God encounter. If we allow God, He will reveal Himself to us in our time of need, but all too often we close the door to Him and shut Him out. We try to fix it on our own. We get others to help. We run to the doctor, friends, counselors, neighbors, pastors, books, seminars, parents, banks... the list could go on forever.

In today's world, we have so many places to run to in our time of need that we don't very often even need God—or so we think. I remember hearing someone say, "When you face a problem, do you first run to a phone or run to the throne?" The question shook me in my boots and began to give me the right perspective. It's not wrong to get help from outside sources. In many cases, that's the way God chooses to help us, but we should never get to the point in our lives where we run to those aids without *first* running to the feet of our Lord.

He is the One who has all that we need. When we run to Him in our time of need, He will see us there and look on us with compassion, like He looked at Hagar. Next, He will direct us in what to do. He doesn't give the full picture, or we'd probably never check in with Him again! He gives us step-by-step instructions to keep us in relationship with Him. This allows us to see Him, who is looking at us.

2 Chronicles 16:9 says, *"For the eyes of the Lord range throughout the earth to strengthen those whose hearts are fully committed to*

him." God is searching the earth, looking for people He can help. Let Him find you like He found Hagar. Allow Him to look at you and see your need. Stop hiding from Him and allow Him to be the one to meet your need and heal your heart.

Dive in deeper on page 144.

8

GOD'S PROMISES ARE NOT JUST FOR YOU

I will make the son of the maidservant into a nation also, because he is your offspring... I will make him into a great nation... God was with the boy as he grew up.

—Genesis 21:13, 18, 20

Sometimes when you're in the desert, you're just trying to get out alive. Survival mode takes over and you do whatever it takes just to make it through the day, without being able to see a future. God's plan is not to just get you out of the desert, but to get you out victoriously and to bring others out with you! God didn't just get Hagar out of the desert; He brought Ishmael out, too, sharing in the promise God gave to his father! God has a plan for your life to affect the lives of others. If you have children, it is God's will that your life so positively impact them in how you thrive in desert times that they'll trust God in their desert times, too.

God wants that same testimony to not only benefit our children, but anyone we come in contact with. God desires that our lives be a showcase for His power, grace, love, mercy, and victory! He is the God who saves. He wants our lives to back up the statement! This doesn't mean that you're going to float through every problem you face, but it does mean that you won't back down, you won't give in, and you will overcome in the end. You will keep your heart soft towards God and protected from the harshness of this world.

Have you ever seen an elderly person who has spent too much time in the sun? You know who I mean: the ones whose brown, leathery faces are as hard as alligator skin purse! If we let God, we can come out of the desert like Shadrach, Meshach, and Abednego came out of Nebuchadnezzar's furnace *"not harmed"* and with *"no smell of fire on them"* (Daniel 3:27).

When I was younger, my grandparents used to smoke. When we stayed at their house, my sister and I would come back smelling like smoke and mom had to wash all the clothes that we wore or even brought there. Make it your goal to live smoke-free!

I'm not condemning anyone for smoking—that's a health choice issue between you and God—but I'm challenging you to live a life that doesn't reek of your problems. If you allow God into your circumstances, He will give you strength to rise above them. He will comfort you in the midst of your problems so you can bring comfort to others. God desires for our lives to help others, like the friends who brought their paralyzed buddy to Jesus. They were so determined to help their friend that when they couldn't get in the front door, they broke a hole in the roof! Remember, God's promises are not just for you!

DIVE IN DEEPER ON PAGE 147.

9

GOD UNDERSTANDS AND CARES

And as she sat there nearby, she began to sob. God heard the boy crying, and the angel of God called to Hagar from heaven and said to her, "What is the matter, Hagar? Do not be afraid; God has heard the boy crying as he lies there. Lift the boy up and take him by the hand, for I will make him into a great nation." Then God opened her eyes and she saw a well of water. So she went and filled the skin with water and gave the boy a drink.

—Genesis 21:16–19

Used, mistreated, and rejected by her boss and the father of her child—lonely and feeling defeated—Hagar gave up. Watching her son dehydrate in the desert was her tipping point. Nothing breaks a parent's heart more than seeing their child hurting. They can handle all the other injustices and go on, but watching their kids suffer can cause their heart to crumble. Parents are brought to the point of collapse at the passing of a child feel the loss that our heavenly Father felt when He watched His son die on the cross.

My heart aches for what Hagar went through. Today there are so many people hurting from divorce. A family torn apart affects each member. When you go through this type of extreme heartache, you understand a little bit of what God goes through. You get a small glimpse of what the Father feels when His love is rejected. You understand a little of what Christ felt when He was treated unjustly and spoken of falsely. How comforting it is to know that God understands the pain of divorce. His relationship with Israel is often referred to as a marriage. Jeremiah 3:8 tells of how God *"gave faithless Israel her certificate of divorce."*

I am by *no* means trying to equate our sufferings with the suffering Jesus endured. After years of singing songs like "To Be Like Jesus," He lets us have but a small taste of what it is to be like Him. Sometimes we don't realize what we're asking for. In those times, it's a good thing to remind ourselves, *"For just as the sufferings of Christ flow over into our lives, so also through Christ our comfort overflows"* (2 Corinthians 1:5). Jesus understands and He cares. Hebrews 4:14-16 says it this way:

> *Therefore, since we have a great high priest who has gone through the heavens, Jesus the Son of God, let us hold firmly to the faith we profess. For we do not have a high priest who is unable to sympathize with our weaknesses, but we have one who has been tempted in every way, just as we are—yet was without sin. Let us then approach the throne of grace with confidence, so that we may receive mercy and find grace to help us in our time of need.*

We truly have a God who understands and cares!

Dive in deeper on page 150.

10

WATER FOR THE WEARY

And as she sat there nearby, she began to sob. God heard the boy crying, and the angel of God called to Hagar from heaven and said to her, "What is the matter, Hagar? Do not be afraid; God has heard the boy crying as he lies there. Lift the boy up and take him by the hand, for I will make him into a great nation." Then God opened her eyes and she saw a well of water. So she went and filled the skin with water and gave the boy a drink.

—Genesis 21:16–19

This is such a sad but beautiful story. It is Hagar's second time out in the desert about to die when God bursts on the scene and brings her provisions of water in a desperate situation. This is also the second time God calls her by name. How incredible to think that the God of the universe knows each of us by name! He sees us in our weariness and calls us by name, but often we struggle to see where His voice is calling from. Sometimes when we're so weary that our vision is affected. We cannot see the provision God has for us. We keep wandering around, desperately searching for something God has waiting for us. Often He's waiting for us to recognize the truth—that we can't provide for our needs. We need to put our hope in God our provider.

Other times I believe God doesn't allow us to see what provision He has for us until we're at the place of brokenness and recognize our complete dependence on Him. If God didn't allow us to go through times of weariness, we wouldn't realize that we need Him. We would keep so busy that we just would live without Him. When we're weary, we're in a good place, because Jesus says in Matthew 11:28, *"Come to me, all you who are weary and burdened, and I will give you rest."* We can rest in the promises of God found in Isaiah 40:28–31:

> *Do you not know? Have you not heard? The Lord is the everlasting God, the Creator of the ends of the earth. He will not grow tired or weary, and his understanding no one can fathom. He gives strength to the weary and increases the power of the weak. Even youths grow tired and weary, and young men stumble and fall; but those who hope in the Lord will renew their strength. They will soar on wings like eagles; they will run and not grow weary, they will walk and not be faint.*

When we are weary, God will strengthen us and open our eyes so we can see the water He is providing to supply our needs.

DIVE IN DEEPER ON PAGE 153.

SECTION TWO:
WATER PARTING

SWIMMING IN THE DEEP END: WATER PARTING

For about four hundred years, the Israelites were slaves to the Egyptians. Their years of bondage wore on the people, and their desire for freedom almost died (see Exodus 5.) Repeatedly God says that He had heard the groanings of the Israelites in their bondage and that He was going to set them free and bring them into the Promised Land to fulfill the covenant He made with Abraham. Repeatedly they said they didn't want to be bothered leaving Egypt. In this case, the Israelites had accepted a slave mentality. Freedom had to be forced on them.

It's sad how people in bondage get so burdened that they rebel against the one who can help them get free. Years of mistreatment can cause people to not know how to live free. Sadly, they often are freed and yet live as captives because they're bound in their thinking.

As you read through the account of the Red Sea parting, I pray God wows you with His power! I hope this helps you to see that He is a God you can trust, that He desires for you to live life free and *"to the full"* (John 10:10)!

Suggested Reading:
Exodus 13:17—14:31

11

ONLY HE KNOWS WHAT
YOU CAN HANDLE

When Pharaoh let the people go, God did not lead them on the road *through the Philistine country, though that was shorter. For God said, "If they face war, they might change their minds and return to Egypt." So God led the people around by the* desert *road toward the Red Sea. The Israelites went up out of Egypt armed for battle.*

—Exodus 13:17-18 (emphasis added)

When I graduated from Bible college, I thought that I was going to flourish so greatly in the Junior High ministry I was leading that the doors would open for me to speak at youth retreats, conventions, and camps all over the globe. I thought I would be like Jeanne Mayo, youth pastor extraordinaire! I saw myself speaking in large auditoriums and even stadiums, if you must know.

I had such high hopes—and I still do! Talking to my old roommate Bonnie the other night, I laughed with her about how our lives haven't gone like what we thought they would, yet we can see God's hand in every step of our lives. We talked about how we don't understand, but we trust that the promises God gave to us will be fulfilled one day in His perfect timing. It won't be the way we first imagined. It will be better! We see how He is perfecting us and making us more dependent on Him through each of life's deserts.

I'm sure if you asked Joseph now, he would understand that he wasn't ready for the palace right after his dream of the future as a teenage boy. It took the compound effect of all the events in his life to prepare Joseph for leading the nation of Egypt as Prime Minister. Fulfilling the dream came as a result of all the hardships he faced. His family would never have bowed down before him if they hadn't thrown him in a pit so many years before. God knew what He was doing for me, for Bonnie, for Joseph, and for all the Israelites. It's the Road vs. The Desert for all of us! We say we want the road, but often we don't know where the road will lead and the dangers it can bring.

God knew that the Israelites weren't ready for the battles they would have to face if they took the shortcut to the Promised Land. God knew that the battles needed to secure the Promised Land would be difficult and that the people needed to grow in trust to be able to come out victoriously and not lose their promise when they received it. The desert may take longer, but God knows what we need to get us to the destination He has prepared for us.

Only God knows what we can handle. Trust Him and allow the desert time to work the character in your life that you need to walk in the promises He has for your future!

Dive in deeper on page 159.

12

Don't Go Back to Egypt

As Pharaoh approached, the Israelites looked up, and there were the Egyptians, marching after them. They were terrified and cried out to the Lord. They said to Moses, "Was it because there were no graves in Egypt that you brought us to the desert to die?... It would have been better for us to serve the Egyptians than to die in the desert!"

Moses answered the people, "Do not be afraid. Stand firm and you will see the deliverance the Lord will bring you today. The Egyptians you see today you will never see again. The Lord will fight for you; you need only to be still." Then the Lord said... "...move on."

—Exodus 14:10-15

The Egyptians were coming in behind them. Pharaoh, who had let the Israelites leave Egypt, had changed his mind and wanted them back. He'd realized that the Israelites were the hard-working people in Egypt, and now they were gone. Why had he let those slaves go? He decided to go out into the desert and bring them back by force. Pharaoh led an army of trained soldiers in chariots.

Fear began to grip the Israeli people as news spread that the Egyptian army was coming to get them. Complete pandemonium broke out and the people started to attack the leader God had given them, Moses.

Unless you've ever been in an abusive relationship, you don't understand how people can stay in one. Sadly, the more unhealthy the relationship, the harder it is for people to break free. Often the fear of the unknown holds them back. The unhealthy thought pattern goes like this: *If what I know is this bad, then what I don't know will probably be even worse.* It's living out the fear-based idiom that says, "Better the devil you know than the devil you don't."

Fear keeps people in bondage. Fear kept the Israelites in bondage in Egypt for over four hundred years of slavery, and it almost put them back in bondage. What if the Israelites didn't keep moving ahead? What if they just gave up in the desert and let themselves be captured? More slavery.

Thankfully, we know the end of the story. We know that God is going to part the Red Sea and they're going to walk through on dry ground, but the people didn't know that. The Israelites listened to Moses' statement about God's power to deliver them. They believed it in their hearts and kept walking in faith to what seemed a sure death: army behind, sea ahead. That's all they could see in the natural, until they saw their victory!

So how do you *stay* out of bondage and not go back to Egypt? I believe that the only real way to see lasting change is to renew your mind. How you think will decide how you behave. You need to wash your thinking with the water of the Word, and soak in the truth so it will renew your mind, first changing your thinking, then your speaking, and finally your actions. Some people encourage you to just stop speaking negatively. I believe that you need to also start speaking positively. Declaring the goodness of God, and how He is in control of your circumstances, will positively effect change in your actions. Keep moving towards the Promised Land and don't go back to Egypt!

DIVE IN DEEPER ON PAGE 162.

— 13 —
DON'T BE AFRAID

*Moses answered the people, "Do not be afraid. Stand firm
and you will see the deliverance the Lord will bring you today. The Egyptians you see today you will never see again.
The Lord will fight for you; you need only to be still."*

—Exodus 14:13–14

Don't be afraid? Stand firm? Be still? When you're in a
battle, with the enemy running up behind you, these
instructions seem ridiculous, even cruel. How could I not be
afraid? Don't you see the enemy coming at me, God? 1 Peter 5:8
tells us how the enemy *"prowls around like a roaring lion looking
for someone to devour."*

On the Discover Wildlife website, I found a great set of
instructions about how to react to a lion seeking to devour you.
I was amazed at how easily the roaring "king of the jungle" can
be shut down. I hope it helps you to see how you need to react
to the enemy's attacks:

1. Being charged by a lion when you are on foot is
   extremely frightening. It is difficult to stop yourself from bolting, but that is likely to prompt an
   attack. A lion charge is usually accompanied by a
   deep growling sound that reverberates through
   your very core.
2. It is vital to stand your ground, perhaps retreat-
   ing very slowly, but to continue facing the lion
   while clapping your hands, shouting and waving your arms around to make yourself look bigger. Most charges are mock charges, so you will
   usually be fine...

3. Hold your ground. Never run or turn your back.[1]

There's a reason the Bible compares fighting with the devil to fighting with a lion! Do you get the spiritual implications to what is said above? In order to stop the enemy's charge from turning into an attack, follow the directions from the website—with a twist. Stop yourself from bolting, stand firm, and be still in God's presence. Then look the enemy square in the eye to show him you're putting your trust in God, that you're not afraid of his scare tactics.

Clapping, shouting, and waving your arms around sounds like a great worship time to me! Worship your way to victory, like they did around the walls of Jericho which came crumbling down! David's enemy was loud and yelled threats of defeat. David ran at Goliath with his mouth open, telling him that he wasn't afraid, that he trusted in God to save and how the victory was going to happen. Waving his arms in the air to sling a stone, David's faith was released and David's enemy was defeated!

Remember: when it seems there is no way you can win, God will fight for you! So be like the Hebrews crossing the sea; don't be afraid, and walk right through to victory!

Dive in deeper on page 165.

---

1 *Discover Wildlife,* "How to survive a lion attack." July 22, 2010. (http://www.discoverwildlife.com/travel/how-survive-a-lion-attack).

14

GOD PROTECTS AND LEADS US
IN THE DESERT

*By day the Lord went ahead of them in a pillar of cloud to
guide them on their way and by night in a pillar of fire to
give them light, so that they could travel by day or night.
Neither the pillar of cloud by day nor the pillar of fire by
night left its place in front of the people.*

—Exodus 13:21–22

*Then the angel of God, who had been traveling in front of
Israel's army, withdrew and went behind them. The pillar
of cloud also moved from in front and stood behind them,
coming between the armies of Egypt and Israel. Throughout the night the cloud brought darkness to the one side and
light to the other side; so neither went near the other all
night long.*

—Exodus 14:19–20

*...the cloud covered it [the tabernacle], and at night it
looked like fire... Whether the cloud stayed over the tabernacle for two days or a month or a year, the Israelites would
remain in camp and not set out; but when in lifted they
would set out... They obeyed the Lord's order, in accordance
with his command through Moses.*

—Numbers 9:16, 22–23

The Israelites always get a bad rap for not having faith in
the desert, but that just isn't true. It's not that they didn't
have faith; they just didn't *always* have faith. Sound like you?
Sure sounds like me!

In these scriptures, we read how the people of Israel were
faithful to follow God's lead in the desert. They moved out

when He led; they stayed when He was silent. Ultimately, God was leading them into the Promised Land, but on the way He worked in their lives to build the character they would need to take hold of and keep the promise. His desire is to do the same in us!

We can learn so much from the Israelites' example here. When God is moving, we must quickly follow His lead. If He does not move out, we need to be patient and stay where we are. Numbers 9 says that sometimes the pillar over the tabernacle wouldn't move for a month, or even a year. Too often we get ahead of God's plan or lag behind. It takes being in close relationship with God to know His leading.

Often God allows us to go through desert places so we can learn to hear His voice and follow His lead. In the busyness of our lives, it's so hard to hear and see where He's leading. It takes getting away and letting things get quiet, without all the distractions, to discern where He wants us to go—or if He wants us to stay put.

God's plan to protect and lead the Israelites in the desert was genius! Smoke and fire signals were used by armies of that day to signify their battle marches. From far off, the cloud and fire would have looked like a large warring army was ahead or behind, depending on one's perspective! How incredible that God put the fire in front of them so they could see, and the cloud behind to block the Egyptian army from seeing them (see Exodus 14). God was constantly protecting and leading in the desert, and He will do the same for you!

The Israelites seemed to find it easy to follow God when His direction was clearly visible—the pillars of cloud and fire. They struggled when they couldn't see His direction so clearly. That sounds like our problem. When God didn't move for an extended period of time, the people fell into idolatry, complaining, or other sins, trying to make something happen. In order to continue running the race to win a prize (1 Corinthians 9:24), we must fight the urge to do something when God doesn't lead, but keep running towards what God has called us to do. It takes discernment to know the difference!

When I started writing this book, I knew God wasn't moving me out of my desert. My step of faith in writing moved me *towards* the ultimate goal of fulfilling His calling for my life, which in turn has begun to move me out of that situation. We must learn to hear His voice when He speaks quietly. Spending regular time with Him, like with a friend, will keep us to recognize His voice when He calls and be willing to follow His lead!

Dive in deeper on page 168.

15

PEACE IN THE DESERT

...there were the Egyptians, marching after them. They were terrified and cried out to the Lord. They said to Moses, "Was it because there were no graves in Egypt that you brought us to the desert to die?... It would have been better for us to serve the Egyptians than to die in the desert!"

Moses answered the people, "Do not be afraid. Stand firm and you will see the deliverance the Lord will bring you today. The Egyptians you see today you will never see again. The Lord will fight for you; you need only to be still..."

Then Moses stretched out his hand over the sea, and all that night the Lord drove the sea back with a strong east wind and turned it into dry land. The waters were divided, and the Israelites went through the sea on dry ground, with a wall of water on their right and on their left.

—Exodus 14:10–14, 21–22

In Exodus 14:8, we read that the Israelites *"were marching out boldly."* How many days do I start out like them, marching boldly, only to cower when the enemy begins shouting behind me, chasing me down? If I don't do something drastic when the taunting starts, fear rises up in me. Once fear is activated, it can start to take over. That's what was happening to the Israelites at this point in their journey. They started off in faith, but gave in to fear.

The victory in getting out of Egypt seemed like nothing in the wake of yet another opposing attack. How quickly they forgot how God had delivered them out of the Egyptians' hands. All of a sudden the Egyptians were back, coming to get them again.

How can you have peace in the midst of circumstances like that? How can you have faith that your child will be well when the symptoms of disease return, when the work issues you overcame rise up again, or when the problems in your marriage resurface? How can you believe that God's promises are true when the enemy is back at your door, yelling about how he's going to take you down? That's the position Moses was in when he said to the people,

> *Do not be afraid. Stand firm and you will see the deliverance [of] the Lord... The Lord will fight for you; you need only be still.*
>
> —Exodus 14:13–14

Ever been there? The enemy is behind you, closing in. People are mad at you and ready to leave. There's seemingly no place to escape in front of you. If you've never been there in life, you won't understand. If you've been there, like me, you know the panic it can bring to your heart.

Like Moses, you too can rise above the panic and perception of the moment. The people *perceived* that they were soon to be defeated. Moses *perceived* that they were about to see God save them. It's a matter of perspective. The way to gain the perspective of peace in the midst of panic is to quiet yourself by taking a soak in the water of the Word.

DIVE IN DEEPER ON PAGE 171.

— 16 —
THERE IS VICTORY IN THE DESERT

Then Moses stretched out his hand over the sea, and all that night the Lord drove the sea back with a strong east wind and turned it into dry land. The waters were divided, and the Israelites went through the sea on dry ground, with a wall of water on their right and on their left. The Egyptians pursued them, and all Pharaoh's horses and chariots and horsemen followed them into the sea... Moses stretched out his hand over the sea, and at daybreak the sea went back to its place... The water flowed back and covered the... entire army of Pharaoh that had followed the Israelites into the sea. None of them survived. But the Israelites went through..."

—Exodus 14:21, 27–29

Now that's what movies are made of! Could you get a more exciting story? Could you have a more desperate-looking situation? Recently released from Pharaoh, the Israelites move out into the desert, thanking God for this miracle. Then Pharaoh changes his mind again. He and his army hunt the Israelites down. The weak slaves run in fear from their evil taskmasters, hemmed in by the raging sea, facing what seems to be their ultimate demise... if it were not for God! God speaks, Moses steps up, and the people move forward in faith. The sea parts and the Israelites walk through on dry ground. Sweet victory is found as God envelops the Egyptian army in the sea that brought the Israelites freedom.

Millions of dollars have been made from movies telling the story of how the Israelites found victory in the desert. First there was Cecil B. DeMille's *The Ten Commandments*, featuring Charlton Heston in 1956. Then, in 1998, DreamWorks produced an animated version, *The Prince of Egypt*. I can remember the goose bumps I felt when I saw *The Prince of Egypt* in a theater! I had read the Bible story countless times, but watching it on the big screen overwhelmed me. Seeing the people's faces when they heard the army behind them and watching them climb over rocks on the bottom of the sea made me realize that it wasn't like what I had seen in my children's Bible years before. It wasn't a walk in the park. Breaking free from bondage was difficult!

The people went through so much, and walking through the parted sea would have been a scary ordeal. I had read the story and thought of them as characters, not real, and for some ironic reason it took an animated movie to help me see them as real! The movie was one of my kids' favorites, so I became well-acquainted with the movie and the book. It was often a bedtime request.

As I write this, I realize that God was preparing me to write this book for many years. Something happened the night I saw that movie. As I watched, tears streamed down my face. My heart longed for victory after being kept low and away from God's promises for my life. I love the ending of *The Prince of Egypt*, when Moses' wife turns to him and says, "Look at your people, Moses... they are free!"[2]

The victory God had for the people of Israel is the victory He offers to us! Don't let fear keep you from the promises God has for you. In faith, move towards all that God has for your life, and you too will experience victory in the desert!

DIVE IN DEEPER ON PAGE 174.

---

2 *The Prince of Egypt*, directed by Brenda Chapman, Steve Hickner, and Simon Wells (1998; Glendale, CA, DreamWorks Animation).

SECTION THREE:
WATER IN THE WANDERING

SWIMMING IN THE DEEP END: WATER IN THE WANDERING

It's hard to understand in our human thinking, but God led the Israelites into the desert. David was led into the desert for protection and refreshing. Jesus was led by the Spirit into the desert to be tempted. Paul was led to hard places, too. All of these people were led to the desert in God's will.

Deserts are lonely and hard. They are difficult to walk in; you can't see very far with all the hills, rocks, sand dunes and mountains. There is no clear path in most places. The temperature is hot, there is little water, and only occasional opportunities for shade.

In the midst of desert difficulties, God promises to give us water in the desert, and He does. From this period of refreshment in the midst of hard times, character is built: character that we can't attain while living in lush gardens. The lessons we learn in the desert make us strong and capable.

Ecclesiastes reminds us that to everything there is a season. Thankfully, the same God who leads us into the desert and gives us water also leads us out of the desert! Just like He did for the Israelites, God will lead us out if we stay faithful! If we follow David's advice in Psalm 23 and walk through the desert, we can rest secure in the promise that He will lead us beside still waters.

The hardest lesson to learn from this section is that if we don't stay faithful, we can lose out on making it out of the desert. In Devotion 24, you'll read of how Moses chose not to follow God's direction. Because of Moses' anger and lack of faith, he chose to do things his own way, costing him ever so dearly. The Bible doesn't sugarcoat these stories and only show the good in people, but rather allows us to see the good, the bad, and the ugly so that we learn from their examples.

We can learn what to do and what not to do. Stay faithful in your desert wanderings and allow God to lead you out in His perfect timing!

Suggested Reading:
Exodus 15:22–27
Exodus 17:1–7
Numbers 20:1–13

_____

_____

_____

_____

_____

_____

_____

_____

_____

_____

_____

_____

_____

_____

_____

_____

_____

_____

_____

17

BITTER TURNED SWEET

For three days they traveled in the desert without finding water. When they came to Marah, they could not drink its water because it was bitter... So the people grumbled to Moses, saying, "What are we to drink?" Then Moses cried out to the Lord, and the Lord showed him a piece of wood. He threw it into the water, and the water became sweet.
—Exodus 15:22–25

Can you imagine it? The Israelites follow God out of Egypt, through the sea, and into the desert only to wander for three days without water. Dry, dirty, tired, and thirsty, they get to a place called Marah and see water! I can imagine the people running to the water, scooping it in their hands and gulping it down, only to spit it back out of their mouths!

I'll never forget the first time my son went swimming in salt water. My fish of a son went running in the waves of turquoise Jamaican waters, splashing about with his friends, when a wave rolled in. He came out sputtering, crying, and vowing never to go in the ocean again! Sadly, he spent most of that vacation playing in the sand, refusing to go in the water.

Bitter water tastes gross, and it doesn't quench your thirst. It only makes you thirstier! We don't know what made the waters of Marah bitter, but we do know it must have tasted horrible enough for dehydrated people to refuse to drink it! They were probably thinking, *Finally, God provides water, but not really!* Only three days into their journey of freedom, they began to grumble, complain, and beg to go back to Egypt!

How quickly we lose faith in God's faithfulness. We don't understand how God can take such bitterness in our lives and turn it sweet. But like the story here, God will do the same for us. He did it for so many in the Bible. Here's a list of just a few of the bitter-to-sweet examples:

- Abraham—from fatherless to the father of nations.
- Job—from boils to Blessing.
- Joseph—from the pit to the palace.
- Daniel—from the lion's den to leadership.
- Ruth—from lonely to loved.
- Esther—from lowly one to liberator of many.
- David—from the king's enemy to the crowned king.
- Paul—from murderer to missionary.
- Peter—from fisherman to fisher of men.
- Timothy—from timid to teacher.

God's Word tells that He wants to give us *"a crown of beauty instead of ashes, the oil of gladness instead of mourning, and a garment of praise instead of a spirit of despair"* (Isaiah 61:3). God is in the business of turning our bitter into sweet!

God was testing the people here to trust Him when life's circumstances were hard and the outlook was grim. So often this is how our deserts look. Life is hard, and then it gets harder. Something looks an answer to prayer, then turns out horrible or bitter. It seems like God didn't come through, and we lose heart.

But don't! Trust Him again and see how He will turn your horrible into happy. It doesn't often happen fast, but when God does start to turn the tables on your bitter situation and make it sweet, as He surely will, it can happen so fast that your head spins at the coming of His goodness! Be confident and know that God will turn your bitter into *sweet!*

Dive in deeper on page 179.

18

DON'T DRINK THE BITTER WATERS

For three days they traveled in the desert without finding water. When they came to Marah, they could not drink its water because it was bitter. (That is why the place is called Marah.)

—Exodus 15:22–23

Picture yourself near a stream. Birds are singing in the crisp, cool mountain air. Nothing can bother you here. No one knows this secret place. You are in total seclusion from that place called the world. Soothing sounds of a gentle waterfall fill the air with a cascade of serenity. The water is clear. You can easily make out the face of the person whose head you're holding under the water. There now, feeling better?

When you first hear this joke, it may make you laugh. You may even visualize someone who has hurt you under the water—oh no, you wouldn't do that, I'm sure!—but the truth is that revenge won't make you feel good for long. In the end, it will rob you of more joy. Someone once told me that drinking of the cup of bitterness is like swallowing poison and expecting it to kill someone else. It doesn't. It destroys you! We can sit and stew about what someone has done to us and allow bitterness to wrap its vines around our necks so we can't breathe, while our offender has a great night's sleep.

The town where the Israelites camped was called Marah. Most Bibles have a note on this verse that says, "Marah means bitter." Bitterness has a way of creeping into our lives without us realizing it. The Israelites said they wouldn't drink the bitter water, but they actually did. They became bitter when they hadn't had anything to drink and found water that didn't taste good. They began to grumble and complain against Moses and

God. They again whined about how it would have been better back in Egypt where they were slaves.

It would be easy for me to read how they acted, judge them, and say how I would never do that, but the truth is that I do fall prey to bitterness. It's something that I struggle with time and again in my life. Deep hurts have opened the door to bitterness, and sadly, I let it walk right in.

Thankfully, when God pointed it out to me I recognized it and repented. I have released forgiveness to people who will never ask it and probably never see that they need it. The condition of their hearts is not my issue. The condition of my heart is. It must be my choice not to drink the bitter waters.

DIVE IN DEEPER ON PAGE 182.

19

IF YOU ___ THEN GOD WILL ___

He said, "If you listen carefully to the voice of the Lord your God and do what is right in his eyes, if you pay attention to his commands and keep all his decrees, I will not bring on you any of the diseases I brought on the Egyptians, for I am the Lord, who heals you." Then they came to Elim, where there were twelve springs and seventy palm trees, and they camped there near the water.

—Exodus 15:26–27 (emphasis added)

One of the many repetitive things in the Bible I take note of are the "If you ___ then God will ___" passages. I'm the type of person who likes things clearly laid out for me. It really bothers me when people don't give me good instructions, and I feel like I don't know what's expected of me. I flounder in those circumstances and tend not to do anything for fear of doing the wrong thing. If God were to give me a master list of what's right and wrong to do in each and every situation, I would love it! I could follow these rules and get it all right, all the time!

Imagine it. You're in the grocery store and the person in front of you butts in front of you. You whip out your handy-dandy instruction book and find the entry for "How to deal with grocery-line butters." If only it were that simple!

The older I get and the more life I live, the more I understand that God is *not* concerned with my convenience or comfort! He cares more about having a relationship with me. That's why He says things like *"Listen carefully to the voice of the Lord"* and *"Pay attention."* When I give my kids something to do and they don't do it, my voice gets louder each time I remind them. Many times they've heard me say, "If you did it the first time I asked, I wouldn't have to raise my voice."

So often we want God to shout out what He wants, to write us a letter, or send a message in the sky. God can and does choose to do those things for us sometimes, but those are extremely rare. More often, God chooses to speak to us in a quiet whisper so we have to pay attention and be close enough to hear. That's what our God wants. He wants us to be close to Him.

I love my husband and children. I love my parents and friends. I would hate it if I had to yell "I love you" every time I saw them for them to believe me. Whispering "I love you" as I hug my grandmother is a wonderful thing, and she hugs me right back.

Are you starting to understand the love of the Father? God wants us to snuggle in close, listen to what He says, and do what He wants us to do, so He can bless us like He wants to bless us!

Dive in deeper on page 188.

20

TESTING, FOLLOWED BY BLESSING

...there the Lord tested them. He said, "If you listen care-fully to the voice of the Lord your God and do what is right in his eyes, if you pay attention to his commands and keep all his decrees, I will not bring on you any of the diseases I brought on the Egyptians, for I am the Lord, who heals you." Then they came to Elim, where there were twelve springs and seventy palm trees, and they camped there near the water.

—Exodus 15:25–27 (emphasis added)

Tests are hard. There's no getting around it.

I have some people in my family who struggle with a fear of tests. When discussing this with my sister recently, she told me about a study that was done on an actual sickness called "testophobia." You can Google it yourself and see that there are people with a debilitating fear of tests, but I think it's safe to say that all of us have some form of "testophobia." No one willingly signs up for life tests. You don't hear people asking God, "Can you give me cancer, a marital breakdown, or maybe boils all over my body? Please test me to see if I'll still trust you." That would be crazy!

Exodus 15:25 tells us that God was testing the people. The book of Job is a recounting of how God allowed Satan to put Job through a time of extreme testing. We all go through times of testing. Thankfully, not many of us are tested to the extreme that Job was, but some are, just in different ways.

Some say that being a martyr for a cause is the ultimate sacrifice, but I think being a living sacrifice can be more difficult. When you're martyred, it's over. There's no more pain and suffering. Being in a difficult situation that doesn't go away can bring someone to his or her breaking point—many times over.

Tests come in all different shapes and sizes. Some come on quickly, while others lag on for years, even decades. Many times, tests follow a great victory, like the one the Israelites had here. They were just coming off the high of crossing through the Red Sea when they had to go three days without water. No wonder they were cranky!

We will all have tests. The question is, will you pass yours? A biblical example is set before us in these verses, in the Israelites, and in the life of Job. If you pass the test, you will enter into a time of blessing. The Israelites, after being tested by going without water, must have stopped their complaining, as the Lord told them that He would protect them if they stayed faithful—and if they didn't stay faithful, they would face hardship. Not testing—hardship. The next event was the Lord leading them to Elim, which was a time of refreshing and blessing.

If you're in the midst of a test, keep faithful. You can stand on God's promise that He will bless you!

DIVE IN DEEPER ON PAGE 190.

WHERE IS GOD?

The Lord answered Moses, "...take in your hand the staff with which you struck the Nile, and go. I will stand there before you by the rock at Horeb. Strike the rock, and water will come out of it for the people to drink."

So Moses did this in the sight of the elders of Israel. And he called the place Massah and Meribah because the Israelites quarreled and because they tested the Lord saying, "Is the Lord among us or not?"

—Exodus 17:5–7

The people just don't see God in the midst of their desert experience. Vision deteriorates in the middle of a sandstorm, and dehydration leaves a brain foggy! Since I don't live in the desert, I can't understand what it's like to lose visibility in a sandstorm, but I do know what it's like to walk through a thick fog and not be able to see the nose on your face. It can be very scary. You feel all alone because you can't see anything or anyone around you, until you walk smack dab into a table. Just because you can't see it doesn't mean it isn't there! Even though we can't see God, it's not that He isn't there. God is often just standing still, waiting for us to come back to where we left Him.

I love reading from *The Message* paraphrase of the Bible. The author, Eugene Peterson, makes Isaiah 30:15–18 come to life! Here's how he puts it:

God, the Master, The Holy of Israel, has this solemn counsel: "Your salvation requires you to turn back to me and stop your silly efforts to save yourselves. Your strength will come from settling down in complete dependence on me—The very thing you've been unwilling to do. You've said, 'Nothing doing! We'll rush off on horseback!' You'll rush off, all right! Just not far enough! You've said, 'We'll ride off on fast horses!' Do you think your pursuers ride old nags? Think again: A thousand of you will scatter before one attacker. Before a mere five you'll all run off. There'll be nothing left of you—a flagpole on a hill with no flag, a signpost on a roadside with the sign torn off."

But God's not finished. He's waiting around to be gracious to you. He's gathering strength to show mercy to you. *God takes the time to do everything right— everything.* Those who wait around for him are the lucky ones.

—MSG (emphasis added)

I hope you read, reread, and reread these verses until you get it. God is with you! He is waiting for you to stop! Wait, and give Him the time to fix everything right. You'll be one of the lucky ones.

DIVE IN DEEPER ON PAGE 193.

22

GOD IS YOUR PROVIDER

"Strike the rock, and water will come out of it for the people to drink." So Moses did this...

—Exodus 17:5–6

He split the rocks in the desert and gave them water as abundant as the seas.

—Psalm 78:15

So often when you're in the desert, you feel depleted, worn out, and left without a way to provide for yourself. You sense that you don't have what it takes to make it through, which can be overwhelming. Perhaps you've lost a job, are facing insurmountable medical bills, rising interest rates, or tuition fees... the list is endless. There are so many financial needs we may not be able to meet.

Then there are the emotional and relational needs we can't meet. Trying to figure out how to provide when you don't have a well to draw from can be debilitating. You feel like you're all alone. Our problem lies in that mindset. When we *think* we have to provide, it is overwhelming, because we can't. When we *know* we can't provide, but *know* and believe that God will, then we are free!.

God is your source! God is your provider! Abraham called God "Jehovah Jireh" when He provided a ram for a sacrifice instead of Isaac. Translated in English, it means "God sees and provides." Let's take a look at some of the ways God provided for the Israelites as they wandered in the desert. In the desert, God provided:

- Financially—silver and gold (Exodus 12:35–36).
- Dry ground to walk on (Exodus 14:21; Joshua 3:17).
- Strength, so they didn't stumble when going through the sea or the desert (Isaiah 63:11–14).
- Clothes from the Egyptians (Exodus 12:35–36).
- Water (Exodus 15, 17).
- Food—manna and quail (Exodus 16).
- Clothes that didn't wear out (Deuteronomy 8:4).
- Feet that didn't swell—even with all that walking! (Deuteronomy 8:4)
- Sandals that didn't wear out (Deuteronomy 29:5, Nehemiah 9:21).[3]
- Shade, by the cloud during the hot daytime (Exodus 14:19–20)
- Warmth, by the pillar of fire during the night (Exodus 14:19–20)
- Protection, by the cloud and fire (Exodus 14:19–20; Nehemiah 9:9–12)

To comprehend how God provided all these things to sustain one and a half to two million people for forty years is difficult. The grocery bill for my family alone is overwhelming at times! You can't help but be in awe of how God provided for them! You can also be comforted by the fact that He did it because Scripture tells us that God is no respecter of persons; so what He does for one, He'll do for *you!* God is *your* provider!

DIVE IN DEEPER ON PAGE 197.

---

3 The only negative of their clothing and shoes not wearing out is that they had to wear the same clothes and shoes for forty years. I know they took clothes from the Egyptians, but forty years of even good clothes is a *long* time! I'm surprised there wasn't a chapter in Exodus about the women complaining about that!

23

ASK THE RIGHT WAY

Now there was no water for the community, and the people gathered in opposition to Moses and Aaron. They quarreled with Moses and said, "If only we had died when our brothers fell dead before the Lord! Why did you bring the Lord's community into this desert, that we and our livestock should die here? Why did you bring us up out of Egypt to this terrible place? It has no grain or figs, grapevines or pomegranates. And there is no water to drink!"

—Numbers 20:2–5

There is a right way and a wrong way to make a request. Any parent can tell you that. When my kids were little, they would whine, moan, groan, and complain to try and get things. It makes a parent frustrated and mad. After all the things you do for your child, and all the things you sacrifice for them, how dare they act so ungrateful for all the good things you have done for them? It makes you want to say no to them. If you do say yes, you do it begrudgingly and don't feel happy about giving in to whatever the request is.

Whining, moaning, groaning, and complaining doesn't make our Father in heaven want to answer our request! Look at the example of the Israelites in the desert. They grumbled and complained so much that they lost the opportunity to enter the Promised Land (Numbers 14:20–23). God says that the people tested Him ten times, and on the eleventh time they pushed Him over the edge. Every other time they were given "second" chances, but now their chances ran out.

For years, I have loved the ministry of Joyce Meyers. One of her most common sayings is "Complain and remain, praise and be raised."[4] Many times over the years, I have heard her voice in my head as I start to complain. Sadly, I sometimes kept right on whining, though other times I am stronger and shut my mouth! For the last years of my broken marriage, I lived like the Israelites: whining, complaining, moaning, and groaning. I had every reason to, and I could have kept justifying myself. God would have let me keep complaining like He let the Israelites, but they reaped the consequences of their words. Thankfully, I listened when God dealt with me about my complaining, and I worked hard to learn how to shut my mouth. It was the hardest thing I've ever done, but it was best to hand things over to God and say, "I trust You with my life. Here's the mess. Please fix it." Those are the requests our Daddy *loves* to say yes to!

Asking God for things is the key, according to Philippians 4:6–9. We need to praise God for who He is, bring our requests to Him, and thank Him in advance for how He is going to take care of us without telling Him how to do it. Then we must think on good things until we see His answer come so that we have peace. I know that the wonderful life I'm living now (including writing this book) is a result of learning how to ask God the right way, in faith, believing according to His will!

Dive in deeper on page 200.

---

4 Joyce Meyers, *Me and My Big Mouth: Your Answer Is Right Under Your Nose* (Tulsa, OK: Harrison House, 1997), 178.

24

KEEP FOLLOWING THE INSTRUCTIONS

The Lord said to Moses, "Take the staff, and you and your brother Aaron gather the assembly together. Speak to that rock before their eyes and it will pour out its water. You will bring water out of the rock for the community... So Moses took the staff from the Lord"s presence, just as he commanded him... Moses said to them, "Listen, you rebels, must we bring you water out of this rock?"

Then Moses raised his arm and struck the rock twice with his staff. Water gushed out, and the community and their livestock drank.

But the Lord said to Moses and Aaron, "Because you did not trust in me enough to honor me as holy in the sight of the Israelites, you will not bring this community into the land I give them."

—Numbers 20:7–12

With a title like this, every man may cringe a little. Instructions... who needs those? The Israelites started out following God's instructions, but they didn't keep following the instructions. They broke out of bondage and crossed the Red Sea. They started out following God's leading, but kept veering from His directions. This led to forty years of wandering in the desert.

The people even rubbed off on their leader. After being born to simple Israelite parents who were servants in Egypt, Moses was sent floating in a basket to save his life. Removed from his family home, he was raised in Pharaoh's household, experiencing a whole different culture.

Later he would have to flee for his safety again. After hiding in the desert of Midian for forty years, he went back to Egypt to set the people free. But after leading the people through the sea, followed by thirty-nine years of wandering and whining in the desert, tired and weary, Moses cracked. The man who had finally learned to consistently follow God's directions got angry and frustrated to the point where he didn't trust God. The people again complained because they had no water. They were thirsty and frustrated and took it out on Moses—again!

God's direction was for Moses to simply speak to the rock and it would pour out water. I'm not sure where Moses' mind was, but I can guess. Maybe Moses was embarrassed to talk to rocks for all the people to see. Maybe he thought, *Well, the last time we had this problem, God, You had me strike the rock and the water flowed... wouldn't it make more sense to hit the rock? Wouldn't that be more dramatic?*

Ever been there? Ever thought God's way seemed too simple? Ever thought *you* needed to do something? Ever thought God's way would look dumb in front of other people? Ever thought it just didn't make sense and wouldn't work... so you did it *your* way, only to find out that you ended up with a bigger mess than the one you started with?

To me, this is one of the saddest stories of the Bible. Moses lost out on walking into the Promised Land because he didn't keep following the instructions God gave him, because of his own anger and lack of faith, brought on by weariness. It's heartbreaking!

The list of heroes of the faith in Hebrews 11 includes Moses. He started out following God's instructions in faith, but in weariness during the last year before crossing into the Promised Land, Moses lost faith in God to provide. This is why the Bible encourages us to *"not become weary in doing good, for at the proper time we will reap a harvest if we do not give up"* (Galatians 6:9).

So get some rest. Deal with your weariness and allow your faith to rise up again so you can keep following the directions!

Dive in deeper on page 203.

SECTION FOUR:
WATER CROSSING

Swimming in the Deep End: Water Crossing

In order to get the most out of the devotions in this section, it would benefit you to read Deuteronomy 30:1–31:26. This is the record of Israel's history right before Moses' death and the call of Joshua to succeed and lead in detail. Then read Joshua 3–4. Read and try to see the people—Moses, Joshua, and all the Israelites—like *real* people, because they were! They weren't actors in a play or characters in a novel. They were real people like you and I.

Sense the agony of Moses knowing, after leading the people so far, that he wouldn't get to lead them into the Promised Land. As you read Deuteronomy 31, try and grasp the depth of Joshua's fears as God repeated encouragement after encouragement to him, saying, "Fear not." That will help you to see how incredible it is that Joshua led these people to cross over the Jordan River, through battles ending in victory!

The more you see the people of the Bible as just that, people, the more you'll grow in your love for the Word and be able to learn and grow from the stories you read. Get excited when you read about the Israelites crossing over into the Promised Land. God is no respecter of persons, so what He did for them, He'll do for you! (Romans 2:11) You will *cross over!*

Suggested Reading:
Deuteronomy 30:1–31:26
Joshua 3–4

25

PROSPEROUS OR SUCCESSFUL, WHAT'S THE DIFFERENCE?

Then you will be prosperous and successful.

—Joshua 1:8

So many people confuse these two words as having the same meaning, but they do not. One dictionary explains these two words in easy to differentiate meanings. It describes *prosperous* as "successful in material terms; flourishing financially... bringing wealth and success."[5] It defines *successful* as "accomplishing a desired aim or result."[6]

Being prosperous is to make money, acquire things, or experience growth in any area, whether financial, emotional, or relational. You are moving forward, moving ahead, and gaining ground. *Prosperity is experiencing growth.* Being successful may involve financial, relational, or emotional gain, but it goes much deeper than that. *Success is achieving a goal.*

The Bible records the history of the nation of Israel's struggles and triumphs. Joshua had been called to lead these people in one of their most pivotal times. God kept confirming to Joshua that he should be strong and courageous and not be terrified or discouraged, for He would be with him wherever he went. The Bible records this encouragement to Joshua repeatedly (see Joshua 1:6, 7, 9, 18; 10:25; Deuteronomy 31:3, 6, 7, 8, 23).

Joshua must have been struggling with fear, but he pushed through it. Just because you're prosperous doesn't mean you're

---

5 *Oxford Dictionaries*, "Prosperous." Date of access: December 4, 2014 (http://www.oxforddictionaries.com/definition/english/prosperous).

6 *Oxford Dictionaries*, "Successful." Date of access: December 21, 2014 (http://www.oxforddictionaries.com/definition/english/successful).

successful where it counts. Don't let the pursuit of money be your goal for success. Enjoy financial blessing if it's a byproduct of your success, but don't let that be your focus. Find out what God's purpose for your life is. Once you know what it is, pursue His plan for your life. Then you will find true success and prosperity in combination.

Such a great combination!

DIVE IN DEEPER ON PAGE 209.

26

BEING CONTENT, BUT READY TO BREAK CAMP

After three days the officers went throughout the camp, giving orders to the people: "When you see the ark of the covenant of the Lord your God, and the priests, who are Levites, carrying it, you are to move out from your positions and follow it…" So when the people broke camp to cross the Jordan, the priests carrying the ark of the covenant went ahead of them.

—Joshua 3:2–3, 14

S cary! The Israelites had stepped out forty years earlier to cross the Red Sea and ended up stuck in the desert. Life really hadn't gone as they had planned. Now God was asking them to do it again! They had finally learned to live in the desert, and now they were being moved out.

There's a time when we all must learn to live in the desert, because we may have to live there for a long time. No matter how long, it's always longer than we want! We want to be like Paul and be able to say,

…I have learned to be content whatever the circumstances. I know what it is to be in need, and I know what it is to have plenty. I have learned the secret of being content in any and every situation, whether well fed or hungry, whether living in plenty or in want. I can do everything through him who gives me strength.

—Philippians 4:11–13

We need to get to a place where we can be content to camp in the desert, but live ready to break camp. The Israelites had to face this situation when they were under Babylonian rule.

False prophets said that God was going to rescue the Israelites immediately. Jeremiah spoke the truth and told the people that they were going to be there for many years before they would be freed. Many of us can quote Jeremiah 29:11:

> *"For I know the plans I have for you," declares the Lord, "plans to prosper you and not to harm you, plans to give you hope and a future."*

Often we don't put that verse together with what God's Word says to the people at the beginning of the chapter. God through Jeremiah told the people to *"build houses and settle down; plant gardens and eat what they produce"* (Jeremiah 29:5). He was telling the people to be content where they were. He was also telling them to be ready to break camp when the time was right.

Don't settle in the desert and just accept that there's no hope, that this is all you're going to have, so you'd better get used to it. We have to be content in the desert, with the underlying belief that God is going to bring us out at His appointed time.

The Israelites must have lived with this faith—that God was ultimately going to bring them out—or they wouldn't have been able to break camp when he directed; they would have settled in the desert. So be content, but ready to break camp!

DIVE IN DEEPER ON PAGE 212.

27

MOVE OUT AND FOLLOW
THE PROMISE

*After three days the officers went throughout the camp,
giving orders to the people: "When you see the ark of the
covenant of the Lord your God, and the priests, who are
Levites, carrying it, you are to move out from your positions and follow it..." So when the people broke camp to
cross the Jordan, the priests carrying the ark of the covenant went ahead of them.*

—Joshua 3:2–3, 14

Can you see it in your mind's eye? Joshua directed the people to watch for the priests carrying the Ark of the Covenant into the Jordan River, and then the millions of Israelites
were to follow the priests holding the ark on dry ground to the
Promised Land. Now that's what I call a step of faith!

The Israelites were to watch for and follow the ark. The
ark held within it God's Words to His people—at that time,
the Ten Commandments and the Law. It was a symbol that
God's presence was with them.

God's Word contains the promises He has for His people.
God doesn't promise that life will be easy, but He does promise
that He will be with us. He promises us that we will get to the
other side in victory—if we follow Him! Aimless wandering
will get you lost. Rebellious living will put you in harm's way.
Fearful lagging will keep you from reaching the promise. You
must keep yourself in God's Word and in His presence to be
close enough for Him to perform the miracles that will take
you out of the wilderness and into the promise.

There's a point in each of our lives when God says that
it's time to move out. It may be a physical, emotional, or spiritual move, but we know He's requiring something from us.

Change is the mandate. It's not an easy time. It's not a comfortable time. Staying in our nice cozy house, in our steady job, or our present relationship always seems easier. Change often seems for the worse, not for the better, but with God directing our lives, change will be for the better! He sees far beyond what we can see in the here and now. He knows the past, present, and future. His ways are perfect, and He loves us more than we can imagine.

In Jeremiah 29:11, God says to us,

> *For I know the plans I have for you... plans to prosper you and not to harm you, plans to give you hope and a future.*

God doesn't want us to change to make life difficult for us. He doesn't even just want life to be better for us; He wants the *best* for us! He wants to move us out of the place we're at and into the place He wants us to be. Wherever that is, it's the best! So move out and follow the promise God has for you!

Dive in deeper on page 215.

GET READY

Consecrate yourselves, for tomorrow the Lord will do amazing things among you.

—Joshua 3:5

Joshua directed the people to go through a ceremonial cleansing to get ready for what God had in store. Does taking a shower make us right before God? No, definitely not. The purpose of the ceremonial washing was to remind God's kids that they needed to keep their hearts pure before Him. It was an act of worship that was purposed to help them set their focus on the need for God to cleanse their hearts and lives.

This reminds me of the preparation a bride goes through to get ready for her groom. We girls spend months getting spa treatments, pedicures, manicures, and haircuts. We spend ridiculous amounts of money on creams and lotions, makeup and perfume. We also read books and attend premarital counseling to learn from others about how to have a good relationship with our groom and put our focus solely on him. We do all this to make ourselves ready for that special someone.

Joshua encouraged the people to do the same for God—to focus on God and set their hearts right before Him. When our hearts are right before God, we open the door for God to work miracles for us. By our acts of consecration, we are saying, "God, I need your help. I can't fix this mess, but I'm putting my trust in You. You do all things well. I'm getting ready for the amazing things You have in store for my life!"

God is honored when we take the time to consecrate ourselves for His purposes, when we set aside our desires for His. It's like plowing a field to prepare it for the seeds to be planted, so a harvest can be gathered. Do your part, consecrate yourself before God, and you'll see Him do amazing things around you!

DIVE IN DEEPER ON PAGE 218.

29

DON'T FORGET

...the Lord said to Joshua, "Choose twelve men from among the people, one from each tribe, and tell them to take up twelve stones from the middle of the Jordan from right where the priests stood and to carry them over with you and put them down at the place where you stay tonight."

So Joshua called together the twelve men... and said to them, "Each of you is to take up a stone on his shoulder, according to the number of the tribes of Israelites, to serve as a sign among you... These stones are to be a memorial to the people of Israel forever."

—Joshua 4:1-7

The memorial stones were to help the Israelites remember what God had done for them in the past, so that they would have courage to do what God planned for them next. It was a time of reflection before a time of conquering the enemy. A time to look back, so they could move forward! They needed to *know* that *nothing* is too difficult for God, because in some ways, getting into the Promised Land was the easiest part of what God asked them to do. The Israelites didn't build the memorial and then stay there for the next forty years staring at it. No, they kept moving forward into the Promised Land, taking hold of everything God had for them, winning battle after battle for their inheritance. We need to refuel by taking time to sit back and remember what God has done. This isn't a time to camp out at the memorial stones and set up residence.

Sometimes people get stuck on something God did in the past and make a settlement there. They reminisce about what God has done and they wonder of His goodness "back when." Somehow they forget to move forward with God and experience all the great things He has in store for them. Their posture changes from feet-forward-and-head-turned-back-for-a-glance to turning-around-and-focusing-on-the-past-feet-firmly-planted-not-going-anywhere. No longer does the reminder propel them forward; it actually holds them back.

Building memorial stones can be dangerous, but beneficial when used the way God desires them to be used. Don't allow yourself to stay and stare at the memorial stones too long, or they will become idols. Fight the tendency to fixate on the miracle of why you built your memorial stones. Allow your memorials to be a catalyst that moves you forward to do great things in your present... and in your future! Don't forget to keep moving forward to the new thing God has planned for you, saying, "You've done it before, God, and You'll do it again!"

Throughout Israel's journey to the Promised Land, and while conquering it, they set up memorial stones to help them remember the miraculous things God did for them. Here's a list of some of the miracles and the truths God wants us all to remember. When you have time, read through this list and look up the stories in the Bible.

Place	Found In	Stones to Remember
Gilgal-Jordan	Joshua 4:10	• God stopped the Jordan River and the people crossed over into the Promised Land. • God is all-powerful. • God performs miracles and breakthroughs. • God keeps His promises.
Jericho	Joshua 6:26	• God brought down the walls of Jericho. • God defeats out enemies when we praise Him.
Valley of Achor	Joshua 7:26	• God shed light on Achan's sin and punished it. • God uncovers hidden sin and brings about loss.
Ai	Joshua 8:29	• God brought about the defeat of Ai. • God's plans for us are good! Confidently do what God tell you to do. When you to your part, God does His.
Mount Ebal	Joshua 8:30–31	• God brought the people to Mount Ebal, as He promised, and they renewed their commitment to Him. • God sticks to His Word, even though it never happens as fast as we hope.

Place	Found In	Stones to Remember
Makkedah Cave	Joshua 10:27	• God stopped the sun until the battle was won. • God can do anything we ask, so ask *big* like Joshua did.
Jordan Valley	Joshua 22:26–28	• God doesn't have favorites, except for everyone. • God has gifts for all His people!
Shechem	Joshua 24:26–27	• God is to be remembered. • God's laws are to be followed.

DIVE IN DEEPER ON PAGE 221.

30

MY LITTLE STEP LEADS TO GOD'S BIG MOVE

...as soon as the priests who carried the ark reached the Jordan and their feet touched the water's edge, the water from upstream stopped flowing. It piled up in a heap a great distance away... So the people crossed over...

—Joshua 3:15–16

Can you picture this scene as it took place? The Israelites have been stuck in the desert for forty years. They're tired and burned out, weary from the oppression in Egypt, followed by hardships in the desert. Through Joshua, God tells the nation of Israel that it's time for them to get to the Promised Land!

Finally, they're going to get there after years of waiting, but there's an obstacle. In order to get from the desert to the Promised Land, they have to cross the Jordan River, and there aren't any bridges. I'm sure they had a feeling of "so close, yet so far." How could they do it?

God's plan was for the priests to carry the ark, which represented the presence of God and held inside the testimony of God, in front for all the people to see. As the priests neared the water, they were simply to walk in. That's it! God's ways are always simple, but not easy. What faith would it take to walk into a large river during flood season? (See Joshua 3:15) What craziness to believe that walking into an overflowing river would stop the water and allow the people to walk through on dry ground? It doesn't make sense. It's not possible in the natural realm, but our God works in the supernatural realm!

Another example of this is in John 2. Jesus, along with his family and friends, were attending a wedding when the family running the wedding ran out of wine. Jesus' mom came to him and asked him to fix the problem. Mary told the servants to do whatever Jesus told them to do. She knew what He was capable of! Jesus directed the servants to fill jars to the brim with water. Then He told them to pour the liquid out the jar and bring it to the master of the banquet, who was astounded at how delicious it was.

Turning water into wine? Not humanly possible. Was it hard for the servants to perform their part of the miracle? No, but if they hadn't done their part, there would have been no miracle.

One of the things I don't understand about God is that He chooses to partner with us to get things done. He doesn't need us, but He values us enough to use us! When God asks us to do something, it's so that we get to be part of the miracle. For the Israelites, it was to have the priests put their feet in the water. A little, seemingly insignificant step set things in motion for God's *big* move!

DIVE IN DEEPER ON PAGE 224.

Section Five:
Water that Grows Gardens

SWIMMING IN THE DEEP END:
WATER THAT GROWS GARDENS

Summer 2010

Listen to me, you who pursue righteousness
and who seek the Lord... The LORD will
surely comfort and will look on with
compassion on all her ruins; He will make
her deserts like Eden, her wastelands like
the garden of the LORD. Joy and gladness
will be found in her, thanksgiving and the
sound of singing.

Isaiah 61: 1,3

Above is a picture of the cue card I wrote on during one of my desert times. I wrote it when my kids and I lived in a trailer and God brought me "water in the desert." Unbeknownst to me, God was putting the seeds of this book into my spirit as I penned that card! I took Him at His Word that He would make my deserts like Eden, but I had no idea how lush Eden was going to be!

We ended up living in the trailer for two summers at our church camp, Braeside. Although these were extremely hard times, we had wonderful times of refreshing there, because God restores! God met each of us in supernatural ways. I will never forget how He miraculously healed my son when he'd seemingly endured too much. After a car accident, ankle surgery, surviving his parents' separation, living in a trailer, and not being able to walk for over a month, Brandon went out with friends for the first time in four weeks. While out, he had an allergic reaction to a bug bite. His face and eye swelled up. This was his tipping point, and he told God that he couldn't take anymore. Brandon asked God to please heal him. The swelling went down immediately! God restored him!

Braeside Camp had always been an escape for the kids and me, but during those years it was a refuge. God shielded us from the harshness of the situation and covered us in His love. There, God put us in an intensive care unit of His restorative power! Now, my Eden is a beautiful house with great landscaping. The lushness of a peaceful, happy, fun, and loving home is the true reward!

This section requires the least extra reading of all sections, but for me it was some of the best water I had in the desert!

Suggested Reading:
Isaiah 51:1–3

31

WHO ARE YOU LISTENING TO FOR YOUR WORTH?

Listen to me, you who pursue righteousness and who seek the Lord: Look to the rock from which you were cut and to the quarry from which you were hewn... The Lord will surely comfort Zion and will look with compassion on all her ruins; he will make her deserts like Eden, her waste-lands like the garden of the Lord. Joy and gladness will be found in her, thanksgiving and the sound of singing.

—Isaiah 51:1, 3 (emphasis added)

Whose words do you want to hear most? Whose comfort do you want to feel? Too often we look to the wrong source to fill our love tanks. As believers in Christ, the King of Kings wants to be our source, but instead we're willing to listen to the words of the court jester and take those to heart. We believe the jokes, and sometimes the cruelty or lies of others.

It takes work to truly look at your life, where you came from, and what you believe about yourself to unmask the lies you've believed. It takes faith to allow your heavenly father to speak the truth about who you are into the core of your being. In *The Message*, Romans 8:15–17 reads,

This resurrection life you received from God is not a timid, grave-tending life. It's adventurously expectant, greeting God with a childlike "What's next, Papa?" God's Spirit touches our spirits and confirms who we really are. We know who he is, and we know who we are: Father and children. And we know we are going to get what's coming to us—an unbelievable inheritance! We go through exactly what Christ goes through. If we go through the hard times

with him, then we're certainly going to go through the good
times with him!

—MSG (emphasis added)

Allowing Him to love you and believing the truth of what your Daddy says about you will set you free. When we try to fill this need with the words, love, and affection of others, we'll always be disappointed. People are human. Earthly fathers are human. They are not God and will let us down at some point, no matter how great they are or how much they love us. They're just people. People make mistakes.

Our heavenly father is different. Numbers 23:19 says,

God is not a man, that he should lie, nor a son of man, that
he should change his mind. Does he speak and then not act?
Does he promise and not fulfill?

What God says about you is true! You can stand firm in what He says.

Dive in deeper on page 229.

32

PURSUING GOD BRINGS JOY IN THE DESERT

Listen to me, you who pursue righteousness and who seek the Lord: Look to the rock from which you were cut and to the quarry from which you were hewn... The Lord will surely comfort Zion and will look with compassion on all her ruins; he will make her deserts like Eden, her wastelands like the garden of the Lord. Joy and gladness will be found in her, thanksgiving and the sound of singing.

—Isaiah 51:1, 3

Some days it's hard to believe we could ever be filled with joy, gladness, thanksgiving, and singing again. Sadly, some of you may have never known a time in your life when you truly experienced such a joyful time. Life can throw us curve ball after curve ball. We are left dumbfounded, not knowing where to turn or what to do. Seemingly, our lives are in ruins.

Each of us gets pitched different curve balls. For one it could be sickness; to another, a job loss or financial burden. Many struggle with broken relationships or broken hearts, while others are plagued with addictions. There are as many curve balls as there are people. No one ever goes through the same struggle as you, but I know there are people out there who have gone through similar circumstances to whatever you're facing or have faced in the past. God's Word assures us:

No test or temptation that comes your way is beyond the course of what others have had to face. All you need to remember is that God will never let you down; he'll never let you be pushed past your limit; he'll always be there to help you come through it.

—1 Corinthians 10:13, MSG

The heaviness that doesn't lift off of us often isn't even a current issue, but a hurt leftover from the past. Regardless of where the sadness comes from or when it came, God desires to wipe that hurt away from your heart and bring you joy. He doesn't just want you to be happy for a day, but to experience a joy that will lift your spirits in the midst of struggle.

Some things are harder to shake off than others, but that doesn't mean you can't get free of them. You may just need to shake a little harder or a little longer! It will take effort on your part, but then God will do the miraculous.

So when the next curveball is thrown to you, just whack it out of the park and run the bases in victory with a smile on your face and joy in your heart!

DIVE IN DEEPER ON PAGE 239.

33

LOOKING TO THE PAST SO YOU CAN MOVE INTO THE FUTURE

Listen to me, you who pursue righteousness and who seek the Lord: Look to the rock from which you were cut and to the quarry from which you were hewn... The Lord will surely comfort Zion and will look with compassion on all her ruins; he will make her deserts like Eden, her waste-lands like the garden of the Lord. Joy and gladness will be found in her, thanksgiving and the sound of singing.

—Isaiah 51:1, 3

Sometimes in attempting to move on, people try to ignore the past, but that only keeps them bound to it. You have to face the past and deal with it in order to move into the future God has for you. Stuffing it down only lasts for so long, and it always comes back up—which is never pretty! Deuteronomy 32:7 tells us,

Remember the days of old; consider the generations long past. Ask your father and he will tell you, your elders, and they will explain to you.

It's wise to surround yourself with people who can help you look to the past. I have taken the time to talk to family members and work through situations that kept me bound. During my separation, I made a focused effort to get wise Christian counsel and deal with the hurts of my past. It cost me, but every penny was worth it! I surrounded myself with spiritually mature friends who were able to speak into my life, pointing out issues I needed to deal with, and also to build me up. I joined a Divorce Care! support group.[7] I was determined to deal with the past and not let it define my future!

One night at Divorce Care!, a lady who had been divorced for over five years shared about how she was stuck in the hurt but didn't know how to move forward. She told us hat she had never allowed herself to cry about her husband leaving. Her life was a mess, and she realized that she needed to go back and face the hurt to allow God to bring healing to her. I'm glad I gave myself the time to grieve right away instead of stuffing it down for years.

Other people start to deal with the past and seem to get focused on it. It's all they talk about, and they never break free of their emotional bondage, even though they may be out of whatever situation caused their hurt. The purpose of looking to the past is to move to the future. Isaiah 43:18–21 says,

Forget the former things; do not dwell on the past. See, I am doing a new thing! Now it springs up; do you not perceive it? I am making a way in the desert and streams in the wasteland... because I provide water in the desert and streams in the wasteland, to give drink to my people, my chosen, the people I formed for myself that they may proclaim my praise. (emphasis added)

Ecclesiastes 3 teaches us that there is a time for everything. There's a time to look to the past, and there's a time to move into the future. It's not healthy to dwell in the past. Once you have seriously dealt with the issues from your past, the Holy Spirit will nudge you; sometimes He'll have to push you and say, "It's time to move on."

---

7 For more information or to find a group meeting in your area, visit http://www.divorcecare.org/.

In my Bible, I wrote a date beside those verses in Isaiah. This is when God spoke to me about leaving the past and taking hold of the great future He had for me.

Two days before my first date with my husband, God had a preacher who didn't know my situation pray over me for all those to hear, saying, "Don't look back in the rearview mirror." He prayed about how God had great things in store for my future, to use me for His glory.

God desires to do a new thing in your life, too, so that you may proclaim His praise! Allow yourself to perceive what God has in store for you. I'm living proof that He can take those dried-up desert places and turn them into beautiful gardens, bursting with joy! Allow yourself to look into the past, so you can move forward into the future!

DIVE IN DEEPER ON PAGE 242.

— 34 —

DON'T WORRY, BE HAPPY

Listen to me, you who pursue righteousness and who seek the Lord: Look to the rock from which you were cut and to the quarry from which you were hewn... The Lord will surely comfort Zion and will look with compassion on all her ruins; he will make her deserts like Eden, her waste-lands like the garden of the Lord. Joy and gladness will be found in her, thanksgiving and the sound of singing.

—Isaiah 51:1, 3

Sometimes my best form of worship is to be glad when all seems bad. Now, I'm not advocating denial. We need to have a firm, realistic grip on our circumstances, but like Ecclesiastes 3 says, there is a time for everything: *"a time to weep and a time to laugh, a time to mourn and a time to dance"* (3:4). It takes spiritual discernment to know when God is saying, "You need to mourn this" or "It's time to stop weeping and mourning; it's time to laugh and it's time to dance."

At times in our journey, the Lord will ask us to worship Him with gladness, and there will be nothing inside us that wants to. Like a stubborn child, we can sit, pout, and fall deeper into self-pity, but really, how is that going to help? The Message paraphrases Psalm 100:1-2 to say, *"On your feet now— applaud God! Bring a gift of laughter, sing yourselves into his presence."* Gladness, laughter, singing, and dancing can be sacrifices of worship during hard times. They bless God and bring relief to our weary hearts.

You can smile even when you don't want to. When your life doesn't line up to what God's Word says right now, remember that God's Word is true and He is faithful. We can trust that He will align our lives with the promises of His

Word because He said it, and He does not lie. The reason we can be glad when all seems sad is found in Psalm 100:5: *"For the Lord is good and his love endures forever; his faithfulness continues through all generations."* Worshipping God ushers in His power to do amazing things!

Think of the Israelite army marching around the walls of Jericho, singing and making music. I'm sure they didn't all feel like it was a good battle plan. They may have struggled to keep a right attitude while worshipping around an unbreakable wall. How could singing and worshipping make a difference? When we bring a sacrifice of gladness, I believe something happens in the supernatural realm that we can't see, and the effect is that hardened walls come crashing down!

DIVE IN DEEPER ON PAGE 245.

35

GARDENS IN THE DESERT

Listen to me, you who pursue righteousness and who seek the Lord: Look to the rock from which you were cut and to the quarry from which you were hewn... The Lord will surely comfort Zion and will look with compassion on all her ruins; he will make her deserts like Eden, her wastelands like the garden of the Lord. Joy and gladness will be found in her, thanksgiving and the sound of singing.

—Isaiah 51:1, 3

Have you ever been to the desert? I travelled to Arizona years ago and loved it! I climbed three mountains and ate at the Cheesecake Factory! The resort I stayed at had lovely lawns and gardens. Walkways were lined with lush grass and manicured shrubs. Exotic flowers and foliage I had never seen before sprouted everywhere. The grounds were breathtaking, but the people all talked about how there had been a drought. The town was going to have to get serious about how much water they were going to be able to use for watering if it didn't rain. They prayed for rain, but I hoped it would hold off until I left!

As we went into town more often and eventually drove through a neighborhood, I realized that only the resorts had grass and all those gorgeous flowers. Most homes had stones on their front lawns, with some little trees and lots of cement. They had no big weeping willows to bring them shade, only desert willows that struggle in drought. Outside the resorts, most everything was taupe.

Growing up in southern Ontario, I've become accustomed to grass and lots of color. Our lawns, other than in late July and early August, have green grass. Trees have leaves of all different shades of green, yellow, brown, and red. Lawn gardens are filled with beautiful flowers filled with so many colors. Fields are full of plants that bear colorful fruits and vegetables—red tomatoes, yellow corn, green peppers, purple grapes, and peach peaches!

In the desert times of life, everything is taupe. There is no vibrancy. We existing, but we don't live. At times it feels like the drought will never end and we're going to die of thirst wandering in the wilderness.

When we're in a desert time, God desires to grow gardens for us! He knows we can't do it for ourselves, but if we do our part and seek God, the waters will begin to spring up. Life will begin to grow again, and color will come back to your life—because God restores!

Until I went to the desert, I never appreciated the colors of the gardens around me. Until I experienced the deserts of life, I couldn't fully appreciate how God's Word could become a garden to my weary heart. Trust God to make gardens out of your desert.

DIVE IN DEEPER ON PAGE 248.

SECTION SIX:
LIVING WATER

Swimming in the Deep End: Living Water

Have you ever grabbed a glass of water that's been sitting out for a day? It just doesn't taste right. It's stale and doesn't seem to quench your thirst. It can even leave a bad taste in your mouth. We're so spoiled here in North America to have living water flowing out of our taps. Any time of day, we have access to fresh clean water.

Tap water is good, but have you ever tasted fresh stream water? That's what you call real living water: water that's not pooled but flows. Living water is the healthiest for our bodies, as it holds the most minerals in it. Fresh stream water is incredible... nothing tastes like it! Water that comes from any stream I've experienced is extremely cold. It refreshes like no other water can. You can feel it going down as the cold water moves into your warm body.

This last section of devotions comes from verses in the Bible that talk about living water. We need to drink deeply from the well of living water. Drinking living water makes us alive! When we fill up, streams of living water flow from within us!

Suggested Reading:
Jeremiah 17:5–8, 13
John 4:1–42
John 7:37–39
Acts 1:4–5
Acts 2:1–4, 41, 47

36

TRUSTING IN GOD LEADS TO BLESSING

But blessed is the man who trusts in the Lord, whose confidence is in him. He will be like a tree planted by the water that sends out its roots by the stream. It does not fear when heat comes; its leaves are always green. It has no worries in a year of drought and never fails to bear fruit.

—Jeremiah 17:7–8

I would love to scream this message from the rooftops: trusting in God leads to blessing! This does *not* mean your life will be free of problems, but I believe with all my heart that when you put your trust in God, He eventually turns things around and brings great blessings into your life! Sadly, too many people give up before they get to see the blessing.

Going through the desert helps us to see and appreciate God's blessings. I can look at countless examples of this in the Bible, and countless other examples in people I've met or heard about. In the Bible, I think most of Joseph, Shadrach, Meshach, Abednego, and Daniel—young men who stayed faithful to God in unbelievably horrible circumstances. Thrown into a pit, a furnace, and a lion's den, all should have died in their circumstances, but by the hand of God, none did. I'm most amazed by the three Hebrew boys who told the king, while being thrown into a fiery furnace,

...we do not need to defend ourselves before you in this matter. If we are thrown into the blazing furnace, the God we serve is able to save us from it, and he will rescue us from your hand, O king. But even if he does not, we want you to

know, O king, that we will not serve your gods or worship
the image of gold you have set up.

—Daniel 3:16–18

Now that's confidence! I know I love it when my kids
speak positively about me, and our heavenly father feels the
same towards His kids. To me, it seems that the dryer and
hotter the desert, the more bountiful the blessing that follows!
The key is trusting God and keeping your confidence in Him!

Think about people in your life who have gone through
hard times—you should have a great number to choose from!
Compare them. Think about the ones who in their struggle
fell into addictions, anger, rage, depression, and unhealthy
relationships, or even walked away from God. Now consider
those who in their struggle fell into the arms of their Lord and
made Him their refuge.

Reflect on the words of the desert wanderers. One group
continually speaks negatively, telling you how they just can't
take it anymore; they're sometimes mad at the world, or just
blame others for their issues. The other group faced the reality
of their situations and also had down times, but they didn't stay
there; instead they talked about how they knew God was going
to work it out, how God was with them, giving them strength.

Choose which group you want to join: the complainers
or the confident. The choice is yours to make, and I pray you
make the decision that allows you to see that trusting in God
leads to blessing! May you be like Shadrach, Meshach, and
Abednego *"walking around in the fire, unbound and unharmed"*
with Christ (Daniel 3:24), coming out of your furnace experience with *"no smell of fire"* on you (Daniel 3:27), blessed as you
trust in the Lord!

Dive in deeper on page 253.

37

DON'T SHRIVEL UP!

But blessed is the man who trusts in the Lord, whose con-
fidence is in him. He will be like a tree planted by the wa-
ter that sends out its roots by the stream. It does not fear
when heat comes; its leaves are always green. It has no
worries in a year of drought and never fails to bear fruit...
O Lord, the hope of Israel, all who forsake you will be put
to shame. Those who turn away from you will be written
in the dust because they have forsaken the Lord, the spring
of living water.

—Jeremiah 17:7–8, 13

I want to be that kind of tree. I want to live my life so that when times of drought come, I never fail to bear fruit. A tree's fruit doesn't help the tree. Fruit is there to feed others. I want the fruit of my life, in and out of the desert, to bless others and provide something that feeds their spirit.

In my research for this book I studied a lot about the desert. I watched a video series by Ray Vanderlaan called *Walking with God in the Desert Discovery Guide.*[8] In it, I learned so much about trees that grow in Middle East deserts. The acacia tree can live through ten years of drought, and as soon as it gets water it will bear fruit again. That's incredible! I want to be like an acacia tree, only better. I don't want to stay dormant like they do and wait till the rain comes to begin bearing fruit again. I want to be like the arar tree, which can send out its

---

8 Ray Vander Lann, *Walking with God in the Desert: Discovery Guide* (Grand Rapids, MI: Zandervan, 2010).

roots hundreds of feet to underground springs. I need to stay connected to the flow of living water.

I also want to look good in the middle of a desert experience. As today's verses say, to have green leaves. Trees with green leaves are beautiful. Trees with brown leaves look dead, dry, and unappealing. How can we attract people to the gospel of Christ if we present to them as worn-down, dried-out, shriveled-up worrywarts? I don't want to walk in a room and hear people say, "Oh, look at her. You can tell she's really struggling. Listen to her talk. She's so negative. She worries all the time."

To grow green leaves, a tree has to soak water into its roots. I want to soak in the spring of living water so that my life is marked by faith, not fear. Our tendency when drought hits is to move away from the Lord. We recoil from Him, and if it gets really bad, we'll isolate ourselves from people as well. This is what causes us to shrivel up and die in the desert.

When I read the Bible, I try to stay aware of the verbs used by God to direct us. Those verbs are often my responsibilities. If you're like me and want to be a tree that bears fruit in a drought and lives free from worry, you need to *plant* yourself by the water, and *send out* your roots to the stream. You can't allow yourself to *forsake* or *abandon* the stream of living water and expect to live without worry. In John 15:5, Jesus says,

> *I am the vine; you are the branches. If a man remains in me and I in him, he will bear much fruit; apart from me you can do nothing.*

So what can we take from that verse? If we stay connected to the vine, we will bear much fruit and *"do anything through Christ who gives [us] strength"* (Philippians 4:13)! We have to stay connected to the source, and the way to do that is through prayer and the Word of God. We have to *put* our hope in the spring of living water. It won't come naturally, but if we make it our practice to draw from that well daily, we will be well watered and strengthened to live fruitful lives in the desert. We'll be able to claim, like the writer of Hebrews, that *we are not of those who shrink back and are destroyed, but of those who believe and are saved* (Hebrews 10:39)!

DIVE IN DEEPER ON PAGE 256.

38

FRAYED LIVES

Jesus answered, "...whoever drinks the water I give him will never thirst. Indeed, the water I give him will become in him a spring of water welling up to eternal life."

The woman said to him, "Sir, give me this water so that I won't get thirsty and have to keep coming here to draw water."

He told her, "Go, call your husband and come back."

"I have no husband," she replied.

Jesus said to her, "You are right when you say you have no husband. The fact is, you have had five husbands, and the man you now have is not your husband. What you have just said is quite true."

—John 4:13–18

The Samaritan woman's life was a mess, and Jesus exposed it for what it was: frayed, just like a rope. I'm sure she hoped each marriage would be the one—the man who would love her, the man who would stay. Each time, her heart was broken, her dreams shattered, her lifeline frayed. She was at the end of her rope.

At this point, it seems that she gave up on marriage and decided to just live with a man. Maybe she thought this would hurt less if it didn't work out. Being without a man in that culture was the lowest point a woman could plunge to. Even women today feel like they're nothing without a man, and they accept the unacceptable in order to keep that man around.

Too many men in our culture feel like they're nothing without the right job. They place their value and worth on the position they hold or the paycheck they bring home. Don't draw from wells that leave you thirsty—wells of people, possessions, position, or power. Draw water from the living well that won't run dry—Jesus. He is the only one who will always be there to strengthen you when your rope is frayed.

My husband Todd's grandmother often says, "At the end of your rope? Then just tie another knot and hang on!" If you know Grama Lois, you can hear her saying it. We have someone to hang on to! No matter how frayed your life may seem with all the hurts, sin, and situations you've been through, know that God sees it all and still loves you.

No one is too messed up for God. Christ saw the Samaritan woman's life. He made her face it, but He didn't rub her face in it. God loves you with an everlasting love. He can take the frayed parts of your life and make them whole!

If your heart has been frayed by broken relationships, I would like to suggest some books God can use to help heal your hurts:

- For men and women, read the book *Love Is a Choice*[9] and do the accompanying workbook[10] by Drs. Robert Hemfelt, Frank Minirith, and Paul Meier (Thomas Nelson, 1989).

---

9 Dr. Robert Hemfelt, Dr. Frank Minirth, and Dr. Paul Meier, *Love Is a Choice* (Nashville, TN: Thomas Nelson, 1989).

10 Dr. Robert Hemfelt, Dr. Frank Minirth, Dr. Paul Meier, Dr. Brian Newman, and Dr. Deborah Newman, *Love Is a Choice Workbook* (Nashville, TN: Thomas Nelson, 2004).

- For women, read the book *Captivating*, by John and Stasi Eldredge.[11]
- For men, read the book *Wild at Heart*, by John Eldredge.[12]
- If you're a man and have a daughter or are in relationship with a woman, I would highly recommend that you read *Captivating* to understand your girl and be able to take care of the tender heart God has entrusted you with.

DIVE IN DEEPER ON PAGE 259.

---

11 John Eldredge and Stasi Eldredge, *Captivating* (Nashville, TN: Thomas Nelson, 2005, 2010).

12 John Eldredge, *Wild at Heart* (Nashville, TN: Thomas Nelson, 2001)

39

LET THE STREAMS FLOW

Jesus answered, "...whoever drinks the water I give him will never thirst. Indeed, the water I give him will become in him a spring of water welling up to eternal life."

...Then, leaving her water jar, the woman went back to the town and said to the people, "Come, see a man who told me everything I ever did. Could this be the Christ?"

...Many of the Samaritans from that town believed in him because of the woman's testimony... So when the Samaritans came to him... because of his words many more became believers.

—John 4:13–14, 28–29, 39–41 (emphasis added)

The five-times-divorced Samaritan woman was an unlikely spokesperson for Christ—or was she just the perfect candidate? She was the kind of woman people in town gossiped about. Everybody knew her and her messed-up life. Even today, people like her are the talk of the town.

Suddenly, this woman of ill repute was calling others to come and listen to the one who could be the Christ. What a change of lifestyle! I can only imagine that she was nervous as she went back into town to get the people. She must have had questions like, "What will people think about me? Will anyone listen to me? Will it make a difference if *I* say anything?"

As she stepped out and told the people about this Jesus, the Holy Spirit drew the people with her words. He used this seemingly messed-up lady to reach her community for Him. The Bible says that when the people came and heard Jesus, many more became believers. The people said,

We no longer believe just because of what you said; now we have heard for ourselves, and we know that this man really is the Savior of the world.

—John 4:42

The Samaritan woman's life made a difference in the eternity of many, many people. A needy woman who spent most of her life looking for love in all the wrong places became a powerful spokesperson for Christ! She came to the well thirsty for water and received living water from her Savior, who in turn caused springs of living water to flow out of her! This woman was wise to draw and drink from the well that won't run dry, the well that would fulfill her need for love—not just for a lifetime, but for eternity!

Isaiah 32:2 says,

Each one will be like a shelter from the wind and a refuge from the storm, like streams of water in the desert and the shadow of a great rock in a thirsty land.

Each one can be *you!* He'll take your mess and make it a *message!* If you let Him, God will take the test you've gone through and make it your *testi*mony. Just like the Samaritan woman, your life can make an eternal difference, if you'll just let the streams flow!

DIVE IN DEEPER ON PAGE 262.

40

NO MORE TEARS

Never again will they hunger; never again will they thirst.
The sun will not beat upon them, nor any scorching heat.
For the Lamb at the center of the throne will be their shep-
herd; he will lead them to springs of living water. And God
will wipe away every tear from their eyes.

—Revelation 7:16–17

What a promise! No more unmet hunger or thirst. No more overwhelmingly hot circumstances. Jesus, the Lamb of God, who is seated in power on the throne, will be our shepherd and lead us to springs of living water. This living water will be what we need! Then comes the most powerful promise of all: *"And God will wipe away every tear from their eyes."* How wonderful that day will be! No more tears!

I wish I could tell you that the last promise in this verse was for today. I wish I could tell you that today God was going to take away all your problems and make your life easy so you would never shed another tear. I could... but I'd be twisting Scripture. This promise is reserved for when we get to heaven, and it will be true there.

While here on earth, Jesus says, *"In this world you will have trouble. But take heart! I have overcome the world"* (John 16:33). Life on earth is hard. There's no getting around it. The false prophets who say that you won't face hardships if your life is right with God are... well, false. Jesus never promised us this.

But don't give up hope! The prophets who tell you to keep on believing in the midst of problems are telling the truth. God has given us promises that will get us through our times of trouble victoriously! Revelation 21:6–7 says,

It is done. I am the Alpha and the Omega, the Beginning and the End. To him who is thirsty I will give to drink without cost from the spring of the water of life. He who overcomes will inherit all this, and I will be his God and he will be my son.

Do you remember the devotion called "If You ___ Then God Will ___"? *If you* drink from the spring that Jesus, the Word of God offers, *then God will* help you to be an overcomer and *you will* inherit all the promises of God.

Even as I write this last devotion for the book, I'm facing a difficult situation. On this earth, we will travel the desert road often. How hydrated we are when we enter the desert and how hydrated we stay while we're there will determine whether we thrive or just barely survive. As we have learned to position ourselves like Hagar beside the water, we'll be able to walk the desert road in victory until we see Him face to face with His loving hand wiping away our tears—forever!

Dive in deeper on page 265.

COME TO THE WATER

Then the angel showed me the river of the water of life, as clear as crystal, flowing from the throne of God and of the Lamb...

—Revelations 22:1

The Spirit and the bride say, "Come!" And let him who hears say, "Come!" Whoever is thirsty, let him come; and whoever wishes, let him take the free gift of the water of life.

—Revelations 22:17

Conclusion

Jesus stood and said in a loud voice, "If anyone is thirsty, let him come to me and drink. Whoever believes in me, as the Scripture has said, streams of living water will flow from within him." By this he meant the Spirit, whom those who believed in him were later to receive. Up to that time the Spirit had not been given, since Jesus had not yet been glorified.

—John 7:37–39

Continually pouring water over a sponge is wasteful. The sponge will fill up with water until its saturation point, and then the water will just start pouring over it. It can only hold so much water. The sponge needs to get squeezed out to be able to soak in new, fresh, living water!

My prayer is that by this point in your journey through the desert you have taken Jesus at His offer, placed yourself like Hagar beside the oasis, and soaked in to saturation. I hope your book is marked up, worn, and almost falling apart after recording so many revelations of God's goodness and His love while you soaked in Scripture! If you haven't, you may still be suffering symptoms of dehydration. If those symptoms are still there, then start over and read those scriptures again. If you're getting hydrated and need some more water, get ready for my second devotional/study guide, or another one that keeps you in the Word!

Don't wander in the desert for forty years like the Israelites, moaning and groaning. Draw from the well, like the Samaritan woman did, and let God work in you a beautiful testimony. When you're saturated, you will be like her! You'll gush with thanksgiving over what He's done for you as you talk to people and naturally tell others how He is the Christ, the one who saves!

My desire in writing this book was to help you draw from the well of living water so that your desert time would turn into a beautiful garden. As you have spent time in God's Word and His presence, I know He has been growing gardens in you. Your situation may not have changed, but your heart has.

The more time we spend in relationship with Him, the more we become like Him. We are blessed to live in a day when the Holy Spirit has been given. We don't have to whoop it all up on our own. The Holy Spirit inside of us does the refreshing work. When we're bubbling over with hydration, those streams of living water will flow through us, and our testimony will impact others for His glory.

Read Acts 2 to see what happened when the Holy Spirit came, just like John explained in the verses above. Christ's followers were changed when the Holy Spirit came on them. Empowered by the Holy Spirit, mouthy and fearful Peter became a bold preacher to lead three thousand people to Christ that day (Acts 2:41). He went from fisherman to evangelist—what a change! When we allow the Holy Spirit to work in us, He gives us boldness to become streams of living water that flow to those who need to hear, feel, and see the love of God!

No longer hard, dry, and parched, you are strong, saturated, and ready to be poured out. Let the streams of living water flow out of you as you tell others about how God has been your water in the desert.

Lord...
Wash over me and cleanse me, I pray.
Help me to apply the healing water of Your Word to
  my life.
Saturate my thirsty soul.
Fill me to overflowing.
Let streams of living water pour out of me
  to refresh other thirsty souls and bring You glory!
Amen.

STUDY GUIDE

SECTION ONE
DEVOTIONS 1-10

1 Losing Sight
Soaking

Deuteronomy 6:18 _____

_____

_____

_____

_____

_____

Luke 7:21 _____

_____

_____

_____

_____

_____

Hebrews 12:1–3 (Key verse: 12:2) _____

_____

_____

_____

_____

_____

_____

_____

Psalm 25:15 _____

_____

_____

_____

_____

Philippians 2:8–11 _____

_____

_____

_____

_____

_____

2 Chronicles 20:12 _____

_____

_____

_____

_____

_____

Psalm 123 _____

_____

_____

_____

_____

_____

2 Corinthians 5:7 _____

_____

_____

_____

_____

_____

Acts 4:19; 7:31; 22:13 _____

_____

_____

_____

_____

_____

_____

_____

_____

_____

Losing Sight
Starting to Swim

If you know the hymn "Turn Your Eyes Upon Jesus," sing it on the days when you do this devotion and let it be a reminder to you that you not to lose sight of the Dreamgiver. If you've never before heard this old hymn, written by Helen H. Lemmel in 1922, you could search for it on YouTube to hear the melody.

The story behind the song is powerful! Read about it on ShareFaith.[13]

Turn your eyes upon Jesus,
Look full in His wonderful face,
And the things of earth will grow strangely dim,
In the light of His glory and grace.

O soul, are you weary and troubled?
No light in the darkness you see?
There's a light for a look at the Savior,
And life more abundant and free!

Through death into life everlasting
He passed, and we follow Him there;
Over us sin no more hath dominion
For more than conquerors we are!

13 *ShareFaith*, "Turn Your Eyes Upon Jesus, the Song and the Story." Date of access: December 9, 2014 (http://www.sharefaith.com/guide/Christian-Music/hymns-the-songs-and-the-stories/turn-your-eyes-upon-jesus-the-song-and-the-story.html).

His Word shall not fail you, He promised;
Believe Him, and all will be well:
Then go to a world that is dying,
His perfect salvation to tell!

DESPERATION CAN LEAD TO CRAZINESS
2 SOAKING

Proverbs 3:21–26 _____

_____

_____

_____

_____

_____

_____

_____

Isaiah 64:4 _____

_____

_____

_____

_____

_____

_____

1 Corinthians 10:13 _____

_____

_____

_____

_____

_____

_____

_____

Habakkuk 2:1–3 _____

_____

_____

Lamentations 3:26

Luke 2:19

Micah 7:7-8

2   Desperation Can Lead to Craziness
Starting to Swim

Are you facing a hardship and considering things you never thought you would? If you are, ask yourself, *Is what I'm considering a mirage or an actual spring? Is it from God or just my brokenness making a plan?*

It may take years, or even decades, for God's timing to be fulfilled, so the best way to avoid falling into crazy thinking while waiting is to get your thoughts off yourself. Get busy living life and helping others to shift your focus from what you don't have to something you do have, or something you have to offer others!

Look for a way to help someone else today. You may need to go deeper than just helping someone for one day and volunteer somewhere on a regular basis. Ask God what He wants from you. He'll be sure to speak when you're listening!

THE BLAME GAME

3 SOAKING

Genesis 3 _____

_____

_____

_____

_____

_____

_____

Try and record as many things as you can about this story, really looking at how blaming others makes things worse. Study the text and answer the following questions:

1. What did the serpent get Adam and Eve to question?
2. What did the serpent exaggerate about? (Exodus 2:15–17)
3. How does Eve add onto God's law? (Exodus 2:16–17)
4. Do people today ever add onto God's laws? If so, how?
5. What did Adam and Eve do when they recognized their sin? Do you ever follow their pattern?
6. What did God do to cover their sin and replace the leaves?
7. How does God's provision of a replacement for the leaves symbolize and point to Christ's future work of salvation for us?
8. What did sin cause Adam and Eve to have to leave?
9. Who does Adam blame?

10. Who does Eve blame?

11. Who should Adam and Eve have blamed?

12. How does blaming affect Adam and Eve's relationship with each other?

13. How does blaming affect Adam and Eve's relationship with God?

14. How are our relationships with others affected when we pass blame on to them?

15. How is our relationship with God affected when we blame others or Him?

_____

_____

_____

_____

_____

_____

_____

_____

_____

_____

_____

_____

_____

_____

_____

_____

_____

_____

_____

_____

_____

_____

_____

The Blame Game
3   Starting to Swim

Blame is a dangerous attribute in any relationship. Pray and ask God to help you recognize any ways that you may be blaming others where you need to take ownership. Honestly look at things and see if you could even be blaming God like Adam did. Ask God if there are any areas where you might be excusing yourself like Eve and blaming others for your bad choices or actions.

4 RUNNING AWAY
SOAKING

Isaiah 52:12 _____

_____

_____

_____

_____

_____

_____

_____

_____

_____

Hebrews 12:1–7 _____

_____

_____

_____

_____

_____

_____

_____

_____

Philippians 2:16 _____

_____

_____

_____

_____

1 Corinthians 9:24–27

Galatians 5:7

RUNNING AWAY
STARTING TO SWIM

In the following verses, note where, who, or what the people are running to or from.

1 Samuel 17:48 _____

_____

John 20:4 _____

_____

Jonah 1:10 _____

_____

Mark 9:15 _____

Hebrews 12:1 _____

_____

Luke 19:4 _____

_____

Acts 8:30 _____

_____

_____

_____

5 POSITION YOURSELF TO MEET WITH GOD
SOAKING

2 Chronicles 15:2 _____

_____

_____

_____

_____

_____

Isaiah 41:10, 13–14, 17–18; 55:1 _____

_____

_____

_____

_____

_____

_____

_____

_____

Zechariah 1:3 _____

_____

_____

_____

_____

Revelation 22:17 _____

_____

_____

_____

_____

_____

Matthew 13:2; 20:21 _____

_____

_____

_____

_____

_____

Judges 20:26; 21:2 _____

_____

_____

_____

_____

_____

James 4:7-8 _____

_____

_____

_____

_____

Psalm 73:28 _____

_____

_____

_____

_____

_____

Psalm 91:1-6, 9-11, 14-16 _____

_____

_____

_____

_____

_____

_____

POSITION YOURSELF TO MEET WITH GOD
5 STARTING TO SWIM

Where are you in relation to the water below? Are you standing in the sand, lying on the beach with a glass of water, or swimming in the water? Draw yourself in the desert oasis illustration below. If you're not like my husband (the illustrator of the drawings in this book) and more like me, remember that stick people are easy to draw! Draw yourself lying on the sand ready to pass out, or in a lawn chair by the water with a tall, cool glass of refreshing water on the table beside you. Or maybe draw yourself diving in, or swimming around, in the water. However you see yourself, draw that, or if you want, draw where you want to get to, and note that, too. Have some fun and be creative!

SOMETIMES GOD CLEANS UP THE MESSES; OTHERS WE FACE

6 SOAKING

Hebrews 4:13

Numbers 32:23

Psalm 119:11

Romans 6:23

Genesis 50:20

Joel 2:25–26

Psalm 18:46–49

1 Samuel 24:15

Sometimes God Cleans up the Messes; Others We Face

6 Soaking

Read Isaiah 61:7–11. Compare these verses to the ones you have read in Devotion 6. Journal about what God is saying to you and what you've learned below.

_____

_____

_____

_____

_____

_____

_____

_____

_____

_____

_____

_____

_____

_____

_____

_____

_____

_____

_____

_____

_____

GOD SEES YOU IN YOUR TIME OF NEED
7 SOAKING

Isaiah 43:1–7

Micah 7:7

Psalm 149:4

2 Chronicles 16:9

Job 28:24; 34:21

Psalm 33:13-15; 18-22

God Sees You in Your Time of Need

7 Starting to Swim

Read Matthew 6:3–4 and write down what good God has seen you do in the secret places of life that He can reward you for?

_____

_____

_____

_____

_____

_____

_____

_____

_____

_____

_____

_____

_____

_____

_____

_____

_____

_____

_____

_____

_____

_____

_____

8 GOD'S PROMISES ARE NOT JUST FOR YOU

SOAKING

Genesis 13:14–18

Isaiah 44:3

Isaiah 54:13

Psalm 119:49

Daniel 3:16–27 _____

_____

_____

_____

_____

_____

_____

_____

Mark 2:1–5 _____

_____

_____

_____

_____

_____

_____

_____

Acts 2:38–39 _____

_____

_____

_____

_____

_____

_____

_____

Mark 10:13–16 _____

_____

_____

_____

_____

_____

_____

_____

8 God's Promises Are Not Just for You
Starting to Swim

"In every desert of trial, God has an oasis of comfort."
—David C. McCasland[14]

Read 2 Corinthians 1:3–11. As you do, think of the quote above and consider how God has brought comfort to you in your desert times. In what ways could you comfort others with the comfort He has given you?

Make a list of the deserts you've gone through, or the ones you're currently in. Remember that God desires to refresh you so that you can refresh others!

_____

_____

_____

_____

_____

_____

_____

_____

_____

_____

14 David C. McCasland, *Our Daily Bread*, "Known Unto God." Date of access: December 28, 2014 (http://odb.org/2005/05/30/known-un-to-god/).

GOD UNDERSTANDS AND CARES
SOAKING

9

Psalm 10:17–18

Isaiah 42:1–9; 43:5–7

Deuteronomy 32:11

Romans 8:17

2 Corinthians 4:10

Colossians 1:24

1 Peter 4:13

Hebrews 2:17–18; 4:14–16; 13:5–6

Philippians 3:10

GOD UNDERSTANDS AND CARES

9 STARTING TO SWIM

Watch *The Passion of the Christ*, directed by Mel Gibson, and journal about how Jesus is a God who understands and cares.

_____

_____

_____

_____

_____

_____

_____

_____

_____

_____

_____

_____

_____

_____

_____

_____

_____

_____

_____

_____

_____

10

WATER FOR THE WEARY
SOAKING

Isaiah 28:12; 40:31; 43:1–3; 49:10 _____

_____

_____

_____

_____

_____

_____

_____

Revelation 7:16–17; 21:6 _____

_____

_____

_____

_____

_____

_____

Matthew 11:28–30 _____

_____

_____

_____

_____

_____

_____

John 10:3, 14–15 _____

_____

_____

_____

_____

_____

_____

_____

_____

_____

Acts 20:35 _____

_____

_____

_____

_____

_____

_____

_____

_____

_____

Jeremiah 31:25 _____

_____

_____

_____

_____

_____

_____

_____

_____

_____

WATER FOR THE WEARY
10 STARTING TO SWIM

Ask God to open your eyes today to see the provision that He has for you. Ask Him to remove any of the obstacles that are blocking or blurring your vision. Record what He shows you here below—and then *rest*.

Read the words of Isaiah 43:1–3, and hear Him calling your name and encouraging you that He will be with you in hard times and bring you out. Find a time when you can just sit and meditate on the promises you've read.

_____

_____

_____

_____

_____

_____

_____

_____

_____

_____

_____

_____

_____

_____

SECTION TWO
DEVOTIONS 11-16

ONLY HE KNOWS WHAT YOU CAN HANDLE
11 SOAKING

1 Corinthians 10:13 _____

_____

_____

_____

_____

_____

_____

Isaiah 30:21 _____

_____

_____

_____

_____

_____

_____

Jeremiah 10:23; 29:11; 42:3 _____

_____

_____

_____

_____

_____

Matthew 6:13

Psalm 16:11;37:23-29;138:7

2 Corinthians 4:17-18

ONLY HE KNOWS WHAT YOU CAN HANDLE
11 ### STARTING TO SWIM

When you're out driving this week, take the long way home. If you can walk instead of drive, even better! Don't rush, go slow, and take the scenic route. Purposely take notice of all the things around you: the beautiful homes, the stores you didn't know were there, the landscaping that catches your eye. Look at the people and see what God would say. Allow Him to speak to you as you slow down so that you can hear Him.

Journal below about your time taking the long way home.

_____

_____

_____

_____

_____

_____

_____

_____

_____

_____

_____

Romans 12:2–3 _____

_____

_____

_____

_____

_____

_____

_____

_____

_____

_____

_____

Matthew 12:43–45 _____

_____

_____

_____

_____

_____

_____

_____

_____

_____

_____

_____

_____

_____

Proverbs 26:11 _____

_____

_____

_____

_____

_____

_____

_____

_____

_____

Psalm 119:11 _____

_____

_____

_____

_____

_____

_____

_____

Galatians 5:1 _____

_____

_____

_____

_____

_____

_____

_____

_____

_____

Don't Go Back to Egypt

12 Starting to Swim

Are there any unhealthy relationships in my life? What do I need to do about them to get them healthy or to protect myself in them?

_____

_____

_____

_____

_____

_____

Are there any unhealthy thought patterns in my life that I need to have renewed?

_____

_____

_____

_____

Is there any fear in my life? Am I letting it keep me bound?

_____

_____

Do I need to change the way I speak about things from fear to faith statements?

_____

_____

_____

_____

_____

God will lead you out of
bondage—you have to stay out.

13 DON'T BE AFRAID
SOAKING

Deuteronomy 1:30; 3:22

_____

_____

_____

_____

_____

Matthew 6:31-33

_____

_____

_____

_____

Joshua 23:3

_____

_____

_____

_____

Judges 6:12

_____

_____

_____

_____

_____

Isaiah 41:10–14_____

_____

_____

_____

_____

_____

_____

Hebrews 13:6_____

_____

_____

_____

_____

_____

_____

Psalm 37:7–9; 118:6–7_____

_____

_____

_____

_____

_____

_____

2 Timothy 1:7_____

_____

_____

_____

_____

_____

_____

DON'T BE AFRAID
13 STARTING TO SWIM

Read 1 Peter 5:7-11. Write down all the encouragement that can help you not fear. Record all the points you can take from this passage to help you to stand firm and see the deliverance the Lord will bring you.

_____

_____

_____

_____

_____

_____

_____

_____

_____

_____

_____

_____

_____

_____

_____

_____

_____

_____

_____

GOD PROTECTS AND LEADS US IN THE DESERT
14 SOAKING

Numbers 9:15–23

Psalm 77:20; 78:53

Isaiah 52:12

Deuteronomy 33:12

Romans 8:31

Hebrews 13:6

Numbers 14:14

Exodus 40:38

GOD PROTECTS AND LEADS US IN THE DESERT

14 STARTING TO SWIM

The illustration in this section is a signpost showing where the Israelites were, where they are, and where they want to end up. Examine your life over the next couple of days, or even for the week. Where have you been? Where are you right now? Where are you ultimately headed?

In the illustration below, the signpost is empty. Fill in the boards with where you've been, where you are, and where you want to end up.

PEACE IN THE DESERT
15 SOAKING

Psalm 119:65 _____

_____

_____

Isaiah 9:6–7; 32:18 _____

_____

_____

_____

_____

_____

Hebrews 13:20–21 _____

_____

_____

_____

Romans 15:33;16:20 _____

_____

_____

_____

_____

_____

_____

Philippians 4:9; 1 _____

_____

_____

_____

_____

_____

Proverbs 4:23 _____

_____

_____

_____

_____

Colossians 3:15 _____

_____

_____

_____

_____

_____

Exodus 14:14 _____

_____

_____

_____

_____

_____

Thessalonians 5:23–24 _____

_____

_____

_____

_____

_____

_____

PEACE IN THE DESERT
15 STARTING TO SWIM

Write out and memorize Philippians 4:7 and Isaiah 26:3 this week. Look them up in different translations. I have memorized them both and quote them to myself when I start to panic in life. The more I panic, the more I quote; the more I quote, the less I panic!

Proverbs 21:31 _____

_____

_____

_____

_____

_____

Isaiah 52:1–2 _____

_____

_____

_____

_____

_____

Ecclesiastes 3:11 _____

_____

_____

_____

_____

_____

John 16:33 _____

_____

_____

_____

_____

_____

_____

_____

Romans 8:36-37 _____

_____
_____
_____
_____
_____

1 Corinthians 15:57 _____

_____
_____
_____
_____
_____

2 Corinthians 2:14-16 _____

_____
_____
_____
_____

I John 2:29; 4:4; 5:3-5 _____

_____
_____
_____
_____
_____
_____
_____
_____
_____

THERE IS VICTORY IN THE DESERT
16 STARTING TO SWIM

Victory in the desert came because the Israelites quieted their fears, stopped their *bad attitudes*, and started listening to their *leader's directions*. They stopped standing in *fear* and started walking in *faith!* *Fear* had them wanting to go back to Egypt and *bad attitudes* caused them to wander in the desert, but *faith* led them to the Promised Land!

I'm sure the hardest part was stopping their bad attitudes. It often is for me! For the Israelites, bitterness and complaining in the desert kept them wandering. Bad attitudes can come in so many forms, like hardness of heart, pride, unforgiveness, bitterness, anger, rage, and apathy. The list is endless.

Fear keeps you immobile, but faith moves you forward! Fill the empty signpost below with the following words to match the direction they will take you!

Fear, Faith, or _____ (your fear, bad attitude, sin).

SECTION THREE
DEVOTIONS 17-24

17 BITTER TURNED SWEET
SOAKING

Deuteronomy 23:5

2 Kings 2:19-22

2 Samuel 16:12

Psalm 119:67, 71

Isaiah 61:3

Joel 2:25–26

Romans 8:28

BITTER TURNED SWEET
17 STARTING TO SWIM

What bitter things has God taken in your life and turned them into sweet things? _____

_____

_____

_____

_____

What is bitter in your life right now that you would ask God to turn sweet? Remember not to tell Him how to do it, just present your need—His plans are so much better than ours!

_____

_____

_____

_____

_____

18 Don't Drink the Bitter Waters
Soaking

Psalm 51:10–11

Proverbs 4:23

1 Samuel 16:7

Ephesians 4:32 _____

_____

_____

_____

_____

_____

_____

_____

_____

_____

Mark 11:25 _____

_____

_____

_____

_____

_____

_____

Matthew 5:7; 6:14–15; 18:21–35 (Key verse: 18:35 hinges on previous verses.) _____

_____

_____

_____

_____

_____

_____

_____

_____

_____

DON'T DRINK THE BITTER WATERS
18 STARTING TO SWIM

In Section Three, Water in the Wandering, the illustration is a suitcase with some stickers on it from towns where the Israelites wandered in the desert. In the suitcase below, the stickers are empty. Spend some time in prayer and ask God if there is anyone you need to release from the hold of your bitterness and give over to God's justice.

Over the next few days, as He shows you people or situations you are holding grudges and bitterness towards, write the names of the people or situations in the suitcase. On the two pages following is a prayer to pray for each person. Pray this prayer of release for each offence and walk in the freedom of forgiveness!

In a few weeks, please send me an email to let me know how God used this to change your life and set you free! Contact me via my website: www.sherrystahl.com

Dear Lord,
Please forgive me for allowing bitterness to take root in my life. I ask you to help me to forgive (*Name person/people*)

_____

for: (*State the offence*) _____

_____

_____

_____

_____

_____

_____

_____

    I release (*Name person/people*) _____
from my judgment and into yours. May I be free of unforgiveness and walk in your mercy and grace. In Jesus' name, amen.

Dear Lord,
Please forgive me for allowing bitterness to take root in my life. I ask you to help me to forgive (*Name person/people*)

_____

for: (*State the offence*) _____

_____

_____

_____

_____

_____

_____

_____

    I release (*Name person/people*) _____
from my judgment and into yours. May I be free of unforgiveness and walk in your mercy and grace. In Jesus' name, amen.

Dear Lord,
Please forgive me for allowing bitterness to take root in my life. I ask you to help me to forgive *(Name person/people)*

for: *(State the offence)* _____

_____

_____

_____

_____

_____

_____

_____

I release *(Name person/people)* _____
from my judgment and into yours. May I be free of unforgiveness and walk in your mercy and grace. In Jesus' name, amen.

Dear Lord,
Please forgive me for allowing bitterness to take root in my life. I ask you to help me to forgive *(Name person/people)*

for: *(State the offence)* _____

_____

_____

_____

_____

_____

_____

_____

I release *(Name person/people)* _____
from my judgment and into yours. May I be free of unforgiveness and walk in your mercy and grace. In Jesus' name, amen.

If you have prayed these prayers in sincerity, you are forgiven, and so is the offender, no matter how you feel! If you feel any bitterness coming back, pray and live your life! Don't let the enemy make you feel like you didn't forgive. Remember, he's a liar—and feelings lie, too!

Father, I reject the feelings of bitterness and stand on my past forgiveness of (*Name person/people*)—————————— .

In your Bible, soak in the following verses as you mark them up to see all the "if... then" statements. Fill in the chart for each section of scripture.

Circle the words "If you, if my people, when you"

Underline the words that tell what is required of you. For example, "listen, do, pay attention, keep, humble themselves..."

Box Around the words "then, but."

Circle the words God says. For Example, "I will, will I, the Lord will, He will..."

Squiggly Underline the words that tell you what God will do *if* you do the above.

Deuteronomy 7:12–13

If I...	Then God...

2 Chronicles 7:11–22

If I...	Then God...

Deuteronomy 28:1–14, 15

If I...	Then God...

Deuteronomy 30:1–3, 8–10, 19–20

If I...	Then God...

"If I do what I can *then* God
will do what I can't."

Hebrews 11:6

_____
_____
_____
_____
_____
_____
_____

Job 1:1–12

_____
_____
_____
_____
_____
_____

Job 42:12–17

_____
_____
_____
_____
_____
_____
_____
_____

1 Peter 4:12–13; 5:6–10 _____

_____

_____

_____

_____

_____

_____

Jeremiah 29:11 _____

_____

_____

_____

_____

_____

_____

Isaiah 43:1–2 _____

_____

_____

_____

_____

_____

_____

_____

James 1:12 _____

_____

_____

_____

_____

_____

_____

_____

20 Testing, Followed by Blessing
Starting to Swim

In life, there will always be areas where we are passing the test, and some where we are failing. Prayerfully examine your life and record some of your findings below. Only include three failing and four passing areas, please. Stay on a positive and passing test score! Let these be a reminder to you of what you're doing well, and where you need some extra attention.

"Examine yourselves to see whether you are in the faith; test yourselves."

—2 Corinthians 13:5

Joshua 1:5-9 ⎯⎯⎯⎯⎯⎯⎯⎯⎯⎯

_____

_____

_____

_____

_____

_____

Deuteronomy 31:6 ⎯⎯⎯⎯⎯⎯⎯⎯⎯⎯

_____

_____

_____

_____

_____

_____

Psalm 139:7-10 ⎯⎯⎯⎯⎯⎯⎯⎯⎯⎯

_____

_____

_____

_____

_____

_____

Romans 8:38-39 ⎯⎯⎯⎯⎯⎯⎯⎯⎯⎯

_____

_____

_____

_____

_____

_____

_____

John 14:15–18 _____

_____

_____

_____

_____

_____

1 Corinthians 3:16 _____

_____

_____

_____

_____

_____

1 Chronicles 28:20 _____

_____

_____

_____

_____

_____

Matthew 1:23; 18:20; 28:20 _____

_____

_____

_____

_____

_____

WHERE IS GOD?
21 STARTING TO SWIM

To help remind you that God is there in the midst of your desert, I want to suggest two things:

1. Listen to Christian music

Mark Shultz's song "40 Days" talks about being in the desert and finding God there. I would encourage you to buy Mark's album "Broken and Beautiful,"[15] or at least the song's single on iTunes. In the midst of my desert times, I have found his music very encouraging.

After the release of *Water in the Desert*'s first edition, Christian recording artist Rachelle Fletcher—from Dallas, Texas—wrote a song inspired by the desert journey God has had me travel through. Often when I speak at events, we sing her song. I'm always amazed when people share with me that they find their own story within the song.

I believe you'll be encouraged as you listen to "You Are Water in My Desert," at www.rachelle-fletcher.com.

I want to open your ears to some musical water in the desert! Enjoy!

---

15 Mark Schultz, "40 Days," *Broken and Beautiful* (Word Entertainment, 2007).

2. Fill in the Stickers

In the empty suitcase stickers below, record places or
situations where God has been with you in the desert,
helping you to trust that He will be there whenever
and wherever you need Him!

GOD IS YOUR PROVIDER
22 SOAKING

Genesis 22:1–18 (Key verses: 22:7–8, 10–14)

Psalm 105:37–45; 111:5

Deuteronomy 11:14; 28:12

Acts 10:34–35; Romans 2:11

Luke 12:22–34

Matthew 6:33

2 Corinthians 9:10

Philippians 4:19

GOD IS YOUR PROVIDER
22 STARTING TO SWIM

pro·vi·sion; noun "prǝ-'vi-zhǝn"
1a: the act or process of providing (see provide)
b: the fact or state of being prepared beforehand
c: a measure taken beforehand to deal with a need or contingency: preparation <made provision for replacements>[16]

Define below what provisions you need God to meet in your life. Place your trust and confidence in Him, and He will provide! When God brings provision, put a date beside the request of when the provision came.

_____
_____
_____
_____
_____
_____
_____
_____
_____
_____

16 *Merriam-Webster*, "Provision." Date of access: November 4, 2014 (http://www.merriam-webster.com/dictionary/provision).

Philippians 4:6–9

1 John 5:14–15

Numbers 11:1–3, 4–10

Numbers 14:1–38 (Key verses: 14:1–4, 20, 33–34) _____

_____

_____

_____

_____

_____

_____

2 Corinthians 6:2 _____

_____

_____

_____

_____

_____

_____

Psalm 100:4 _____

_____

_____

_____

_____

_____

_____

Mark 14:36 _____

_____

_____

_____

_____

_____

_____

_____

_____

ASK THE RIGHT WAY
23 STARTING TO SWIM

Numbers 13 records the story of how God told Moses to choose twelve men so they could spy out the Promised Land. All God wanted them to do was go and see how good it was and come back to tell the people about the land He was giving to the Israelites. God promised them that *He* was giving it to them.

Compare Joshua and Caleb to the other spies in the record of Numbers 13:1–14:38.

Compare their reports on what the Promised Land was like (13:27; 14:6–8). _____

_____

_____

_____

_____

Compare their perspectives on the strength of the people (13:28–33, 14:9). _____

_____

_____

_____

_____

Compare the results of their words (14:36–38). _____

_____

_____

_____

_____

_____

24 KEEP FOLLOWING THE INSTRUCTIONS
SOAKING

Hebrews 11:23–28

Galatians 5:1

Galatians 5:5–15

Galatians 5:22–25; 6:9

1 Corinthians 9:24–27

2 Corinthians 11:26–33

Acts 1:8; 4:33; 20:22–24

Colossians 1:21–23; 2:7

Hebrews 12:1–3

Keep Following the Instructions
24 Starting to Swim

Each person is rejuvenated by different things. What fills up your energy tank? Some people need time alone to refuel while others need time out with people. So what's your rhythm? In the lines below, list things you can do to help rid yourself of weariness, anger, and lack of faith._____

_____

_____

_____

_____

_____

What instruction do you need to follow through on with God? If you don't have one, ask Him to give you one!_____

_____

_____

_____

_____

_____

Take time this week to do some of the things that will energize you so that you can *keep* following God's plan for your life and one day walk in your Promised Land!

SECTION FOUR
DEVOTIONS 25-30

PROSPEROUS OR SUCCESSFUL, WHAT'S THE DIFFERENCE?

25 SOAKING

Genesis 24:21 _____

Genesis 24:30:43; 39:2 _____

Deuteronomy 30:5–10 _____

Deuteronomy 30:15–16 _____

Judges 18:5 _____

_____

_____

_____

_____

_____

_____

Job 8:7; 42:10 _____

_____

_____

_____

_____

_____

_____

Isaiah 48:15 _____

_____

_____

_____

_____

_____

_____

Psalm 35:27[17] _____

_____

_____

_____

_____

_____

_____

17 This is great in the King James Version (KJV).

Prosperous or Successful, What's the Difference?

25 Starting to Swim

Read 1 Chronicles 4:10. This is the Prayer of Jabez. The prayer was made famous in the last decade by Bruce Wilkinson's book, called *The Prayer of Jabez*.[18] If you haven't read it, I highly recommend you do! This book will help you to grow in a deeper understanding of how God desires for you to prosper.

Write out 1 Chronicles 4:10 below. Pray this prayer daily and see how God will bring prosperity and success into your life.

18 Bruce Wilkinson, *The Prayer of Jabez* (Sisters, OR: Multnomah Publishers, 2000).

26 · Being Content, but Ready to Break Camp
Soaking

Psalm 23:4 _____

_____

_____

_____

_____

_____

Isaiah 26:3–4 _____

_____

_____

_____

_____

_____

Isaiah 30:18 _____

_____

_____

_____

_____

_____

_____

Philippians 4:11–13 _____

_____

_____

_____

_____

_____

_____

1 Timothy 6:6–10 ⸻

⸻

Hebrews 13:5 ⸻

⸻

Proverbs 19:23 ⸻

⸻

Luke 3:14 ⸻

⸻

James 1:1[19] ⸻

⸻

19 This is particularly good in *The Message* paraphrase.

26 BEING CONTENT, BUT READY TO BREAK CAMP
STARTING TO SWIM

So, what is your desert mentality? Are you just camping, waiting for marching orders, or have you settled in your circumstance?

_____

_____

Write out Philippians 4:11-13 and put verse 13 in BOLD—or highlight it! _____

_____

_____

_____

_____

Write out a sentence about how you believe in faith that God is going to bring you out of the desert. Read it to yourself whenever you need to be encouraged to keep believing! _____

_____

_____

_____

> "Everything will work out in the end.
> If it's not working out, it's not the end!"
> —Author Unknown

Genesis 15:18–21 _____

_____
_____
_____
_____
_____
_____
_____

Exodus 14:15; 25:8–21; 40:20 _____

_____
_____
_____
_____
_____
_____
_____

Deuteronomy 10:1–5; 31:9 _____

_____
_____
_____
_____
_____
_____

Psalm 145:13; 89:34; 146:6 _____

_____
_____

Isaiah 50:7

Habakkuk 2:2-3

Hebrews 6:13-15, 18

Move Out and Follow the Promise
27 Starting to Swim

The promise God made to the Israelites is recorded in Joshua 1:2–3: *"get ready to cross the Jordan River into the land I am about to give to them—to the Israelites. I will give you every place you set your foot, as I promised Moses."* The passage goes on to state the actual physical boundaries God had for them.

In the journal section below, record what God has promised you personally or promises from His Word. Describe where you're going to go and who you're going to be when you get there! Fill in the signpost below as to where you are "moving out" to!

_____

_____

_____

_____

_____

_____

_____

_____

Isaiah 40:3–5 _____

_____

_____

_____

_____

_____

_____

_____

_____

_____

_____

_____

Exodus 19:10–11 _____

_____

_____

_____

_____

_____

_____

_____

_____

_____

_____

Joel 2:15–19 _____

_____

_____

_____

_____

_____

_____

_____

Joel 2:25–26 _____

_____

_____

_____

_____

_____

_____

_____

_____

Jeremiah 1:17–19 _____

_____

_____

_____

_____

_____

_____

Isaiah 52:11 _____

_____

_____

_____

_____

_____

_____

_____

GET READY
STARTING TO SWIM

28

If consecration means "dedicated to a sacred purpose,"[20] what act of consecration can you do today to open the door for God to do amazing things in your life? Wait quietly before the Lord and let him reveal to you what it should be. Expect *amazing* things! Don't forget to write me and let me know about your miracle!

_____

_____

_____

_____

_____

_____

_____

_____

_____

_____

_____

_____

---

20 *Merriam-Webster*, "Consecrate." Date of access: December 21, 2014 (http://www.merriam-webster.com/dictionary/consecrate).

29 DON'T FORGET
SOAKING

Psalm 42:5–6; 119 _____

_____

_____

_____

_____

_____

_____

_____

Lamentations 3:21–23 _____

_____

_____

_____

_____

_____

_____

Deuteronomy 7:18 _____

_____

_____

_____

_____

_____

_____

_____

29 DON'T FORGET
STARTING TO SWIM

Remembering gives us hope for the future. It changes our focus from looking at life with a cup half-empty to a cup half-full—or could yours be overflowing with God's goodness?

In the cup below, record at least five times that God took care of you in the past. Continue adding to this cup as God blesses you. Eventually the picture will be overflowing with reminders of His goodness and His ability to be who and what you need! Drink from this cup of remembrance regularly to help you believe and hope!

> *"Yet this I call to mind and therefore I have hope: Because of the Lord's great love we are not consumed, for his compassions never fail. They are new every morning; great is your faithfulness."*
>
> —Lamentations 3:21–23

John 2:1–11 _____

_____
_____
_____
_____
_____
_____
_____
_____
_____
_____
_____

Zechariah 4:6 _____

_____
_____
_____
_____
_____
_____
_____
_____
_____
_____
_____
_____
_____

Zechariah 4:8-10 _____

_____

_____

_____

_____

_____

_____

_____

_____

_____

_____

_____

_____

_____

_____

_____

Joshua 3:13, 15-17 _____

_____

_____

_____

_____

_____

_____

_____

_____

_____

_____

_____

_____

_____

_____

_____

MY LITTLE STEP LEADS TO GOD'S BIG MOVE
30 STARTING TO SWIM

God will not do our part, and we cannot do His part. The exciting thing is that our part really is simple—not always easy, but simple.

What simple "faith step" is God asking you to take today in moving towards His goal for your life? Write it down, and then go do it! Remember: your little step leads to God's *big* move!

_____

_____

_____

_____

_____

_____

_____

_____

_____

_____

_____

_____

_____

SECTION FIVE
DEVOTIONS 31-35

WHO ARE YOU LISTENING TO FOR YOUR WORTH?

Ask yourself, *who* are you listening to for your self-worth? Pray about it, and ask the Holy Spirit to help you recognize some of the "court jesters" you have listened to, and the lies you have believed. You may have to think about this for a day or two, or even a week, to allow the Holy Spirit time to reveal the truth to you. You may start with a name or two, then keep adding to the list. Some may be people you know, and other sources may be magazines, videos, or television shows.

Please do not rush this step, as I believe it is critical for you to understand some of the false things you have believed about yourself. Allow the Holy Spirit to point them out in order for you to be ready for the next step of replacing lies with truth. Record the source of your false beliefs and the lies that were believed.

Source	Lie Believed

31 WHO ARE YOU LISTENING TO FOR YOUR WORTH?
SOAKING/STARTING TO SWIM

Once you have thought about and answered the questions, take the next step.

When you receive Christ into your heart and life, your position with God is immediately changed. Getting your mind to catch up often takes more time!

In the following days or weeks, take the time to read and soak in these scriptures that tell about our position in Christ at salvation. They will help you to hear what God says about you, if you listen with your spirit. As you read and journal about them, ask your Daddy to let the truth of who He says you are sink in and penetrate your mind and belief system. Ask Him to renew your mind with His truths (Romans 12:2).

In the journal lines below, record declarations for you to speak over your life. Here are some suggested ways to start your declarations:

I am _____.
I am valuable because _____.
I am valued as _____.
I have significance because _____.
I have _____.
I am accepted _____.
I am secure because _____.
I am valued because _____.
I am _____ since _____.
I am protected _____.
I belong _____.
I am loved by God because _____.
I am _____, therefore I have _____
        (significance, value, worth...).

End your statements with exclamation marks, so when you declare them you do so with emphasis!

Deuteronomy 28:1–6 _____

_____

_____

_____

_____

_____

Psalm 45:11 _____

_____

_____

_____

_____

Matthew 5:13–14 _____

_____

_____

_____

_____

Mark 16:17–18 _____

_____

_____

_____

_____

John 1:12 _____

_____

_____

_____

_____

_____

_____

John 15:1, 5, 15–16 _____

_____

_____

_____

_____

_____

Acts 1:8 _____

_____

_____

_____

_____

_____

Romans 5:1 _____

_____

_____

_____

_____

_____

Romans 6:11 _____

_____

_____

_____

_____

_____

Romans 8 (Key verses: 1–2, 14–17, 28, 31–39) _____

_____

_____

_____

1 Corinthians 3:16

1 Corinthians 6:19–20

1 Corinthians 12:27

1 Corinthians 15:57

2 Corinthians 1:21–22

_____

_____

_____

_____

2 Corinthians 3:38_____

_____

_____

_____

_____

_____

2 Corinthians 5:17–21_____

_____

_____

_____

_____

_____

2 Corinthians 6:1_____

_____

_____

_____

_____

_____

2 Corinthians 12:27_____

_____

_____

_____

_____

_____

2 Timothy 1:7_____

_____

_____

Galatians 3:26–4:7

Ephesians 1:1, 4–5, 7, 11

Ephesians 2:6, 10, 18–20

Ephesians 3:12

Philippians 1:6

Philippians 3:20

Philippians 4:7, 13

Colossians 1:14

Colossians 2:10

Colossians 3:3

James 1:17–18

1 John 5:18

If self-worth is a struggle for you, I encourage you to read Robert S. McGee's book, *The Search for Significance*[21] and complete the workbook questions inside. God used this book powerfully in my life to break down the lies I was believing and wash them away with the water of the Word.

---

21 Robert S. McGee, *The Search for Significance* (Nashville, TN: Thomas Nelson, 2003).

Songs of Songs 2:11–12 _____

_____
_____
_____
_____
_____
_____
_____

Hebrews 11:6 _____

_____
_____
_____
_____
_____
_____
_____

James 4:7–10 _____

_____
_____
_____
_____
_____
_____

Matthew 5:6 _____

_____
_____

Isaiah 42:10–13

Isaiah 54:10–15 (Key verses 54:11–12, 14)

Isaiah 55:12–13

32 Pursuing God Brings Joy in the Desert
Starting to Swim

Write out three things you're thankful for:

_____

_____

_____

What is your favorite comedy film?

_____

Who is your funniest friend? Tell one thing about them.

_____

What is your favorite Christian singer or band?

_____

What is your favorite worship song at church?

_____

What is something you can do to pursue joy, gladness, and the sound of singing?

_____

_____

_____

Deuteronomy 4:32 _____

_____
_____
_____
_____
_____

Deuteronomy 32:7 _____

_____
_____
_____
_____
_____

Psalm 77:5 _____

_____
_____
_____
_____
_____

Jeremiah 6:16 _____

_____
_____
_____
_____
_____

Job 8:8 _____

_____

_____

_____

_____

_____

_____

Proverbs 15:9_____

_____

_____

_____

_____

Isaiah 46:9_____

_____

_____

_____

_____

2 Corinthians 5:17_____

_____

_____

_____

_____

Isaiah 43:18–21_____

_____

_____

_____

_____

_____

_____

LOOKING TO THE PAST,
SO YOU CAN MOVE INTO THE FUTURE

33 STARTING TO SWIM

Ask the Holy Spirit—*"the Spirit of truth,"* according to John 16:13—to reveal to you what season you are in right now: looking to the past, or moving to the future. Sometimes you may be in a bit of both, but most often you are in one or the other, needing to deal with a past issue or needing to move into what God has for your future.

After you've spent time waiting on the Lord to bring to light what needs to be seen, journal about the following questions.

What is holding you captive, and what has been helpful from your past? Record your thoughts below.

_____

_____

_____

What is the "new thing" God is doing, or going to do, in your life? Ask the Holy Spirit to help you perceive it.

_____

_____

_____

_____

_____

_____

_____

_____

Believe God to take your ruins and make
them beautiful gardens filled with joy!

DON'T WORRY, BE HAPPY
34 SOAKING

Psalm 100:2-5 _____

_____

_____

_____

_____

_____

Philippians 1:6 _____

_____

_____

_____

_____

_____

Acts 16:22-26 _____

_____

_____

_____

_____

_____

Proverbs 17:22 _____

_____

_____

_____

_____

_____

_____

_____

Psalm 27:6; 50:14, 23; 54:6; 107:22; 126:2 _____

_____

_____

_____

_____

_____

_____

_____

Jeremiah 33:10–14 _____

_____

_____

_____

_____

_____

Hebrews 13:15 _____

_____

_____

_____

_____

_____

_____

34 DON'T WORRY, BE HAPPY
STARTING TO SWIM

Make a choice to be happy today. Put on the *"garment of praise"* (Isaiah 61:3).

Go to the mirror and smile until you make yourself laugh. Then you can maybe stir up a real smile.

Sing and do the actions for that '80s worship song "We Bring the Sacrifice of Praise," and keep doing it until you laugh at yourself! It really is a God-inspired song; it's just not easy to do some days.[22]

To learn the story behind the song and how it has impacted so many, go to Kirk and Deby Dearman's website.[23] The Dearmans have experienced great joy for their sacrifice of praise.

"It's the praising life that honors me.
As soon as you set your foot on the Way,
I'll show you my salvation."
—Psalm 50:23, MSG

22 I found a great YouTube rendition of this song which you may want to sing along with (http://www.youtube.com/watch?v=Zs_WEQuEo8U). There are so many other renditions of this song on YouTube. You can check them out to find one that best suits for musical tastes.

23 *Art, Music, Inspiration,* "We Bring the Sacrifice of Praise." Date of access: December 10, 2014 (www.cometothequiet.com/sacofpraise.cfm).

GARDENS IN THE DESERT
SOAKING

Genesis 2:8–15 _____

_____
_____
_____
_____
_____
_____
_____

Joel 2:3, 25–27 _____

_____
_____
_____
_____
_____
_____

Ezekiel 36:33–36 (Key verse: 36:35) _____

_____
_____
_____
_____
_____
_____

Isaiah 58:11 _____

_____
_____

Songs of Songs 4:15

2 Corinthians 5:17

Isaiah 32:15–18

GARDENS IN THE DESERT
35 STARTING TO SWIM

If you live in a climate where there are lots of colorful plants, go for a walk in your neighborhood and really take in the beauty of it all. If you live near a botanical garden, you could visit it. You could go into a florist shop and smell the roses! If you live in the desert... drive through a resort. If it's winter, go online and look at pictures of gardens. If you're artistic, draw a flower or some plants; I left you some space below.

Try and remember what it's like to smell flowers and feel the grass beneath your feet. Buy some cut flowers and display them in your home to see, smell, and touch.

Whenever you are in a desert time, do things like this to remind yourself that God desires to spring up a garden in the midst of your desert!

SECTION SIX
DEVOTIONS 36-40

Proverbs 3:5–6, 19:23

_____

_____

_____

_____

_____

_____

_____

Habakkuk 3:17–18

_____

_____

_____

_____

_____

_____

_____

Romans 10:11, 15:13

_____

_____

_____

_____

_____

_____

_____

_____

1 Peter 1:1–11[24]_____

_____

_____

_____

_____

_____

_____

_____

_____

_____

_____

Psalm 20:7–8; 118:5–12_____

_____

_____

_____

_____

_____

_____

_____

_____

_____

Daniel 3, 6_____

_____

_____

_____

_____

_____

_____

_____

_____

_____

_____

24 I love how this is written in *The Message* paraphrase, especially 1:11.

TRUSTING IN GOD LEADS TO BLESSING
36 STARTING TO SWIM

Song of Solomon 8:5 says, *"Who is this coming up from the desert leaning on her lover?"* The relationship in the Song of Solomon between the Shunamite woman and Solomon are to represent our relationship with Christ. You can come *up* out of the wilderness and not be beaten down if you lean on the one you love!

Have a campfire or set a fire burning in your fireplace with someone. Enjoy your time. Afterward, smell your clothes and your hair. Let it be a reminder to you that God desires to be with you and bring you out of your fiery circumstances with no smell of fire on you. If you can't do this, remember a time of being at a campfire and the smell of your clothes.

DON'T SHRIVEL UP!
37 SOAKING

Isaiah 40:29–31 _____

_____

_____

_____

_____

_____

_____

Hebrews 10:35–39 _____

_____

_____

_____

_____

_____

_____

Psalm 16:8–10 _____

_____

_____

_____

_____

_____

_____

Psalm 118:13–16 _____

_____

_____

_____

_____

_____

Psalm 42:5–6, 11; 43:5

Psalm 119:49–50

2 Samuel 22:33–37

Galatians 5:22–26

Don't Shrivel Up!
37 Starting to Swim

When my children were little, I loved taking them to an orchard to pick apples. They are my favorite fruit and the most delicious smell I know! Each year I also took them to pick out pumpkins for Thanksgiving decorations, and sometimes we would go to a pumpkin patch. Oh how they loved it! Over the years, we picked apples, pears, peaches, oranges, plums... the list of fruits could go on.

Imagine you are a tree and your leaves are a lush green. What fruit would be growing under those leaves? What fruit do you want your life to produce? Write it down.

_____

_____

_____

_____

_____

_____

_____

_____

_____

_____

_____

"But the fruit of the Spirit is love, joy, peace, patience, kindness, goodness, faithfulness, gentleness and self-control."
—Galatians 5:22–23

Jeremiah 2:13 _____

_____

_____

_____

_____

_____

Hebrews 13:5

> *...for He [God] Himself has said, I will not in any way*
> *fail you nor give you up nor leave you without support. [I*
> *will] not, [I will] not, [I will] not in any degree leave you*
> *helpless nor forsake nor let [you] down (relax My hold on*
> *you)! [Assuredly not!]*
>
> —Hebrews 13:5, AMP

Write out Hebrews 13:5 from your version of the Bible:

_____

_____

_____

_____

_____

_____

John 3:16 _____

_____

_____

_____

_____

John 6:35 _____

_____
_____
_____
_____
_____
_____
_____

Romans 5:16 _____

_____
_____
_____
_____
_____
_____
_____

Romans 8:1 _____

_____
_____
_____
_____
_____
_____
_____

Romans 8:35–39 _____

_____
_____
_____
_____
_____
_____
_____

FRAYED LIVES
38 STARTING TO SWIM

What are some of the events that have "frayed" your life?

_____

_____

_____

_____

Are there any *people* in your life who you are trying to "draw" from more than God? If so, who?_____

_____

_____

Are there any *things* in your life that you are trying to "draw" from more than God? If so, what?_____

_____

_____

How do you know that God will never leave
you or forsake you?_____

_____

_____

_____

_____

_____

_____

_____

_____

_____

_____

Isaiah 32:2 _____

_____

_____

_____

_____

_____

_____

Isaiah 58:11 _____

_____

_____

_____

_____

_____

Jeremiah 31:25 _____

_____

_____

_____

_____

_____

Matthew 28:19; Mark 16:15 _____

_____

_____

_____

_____

John 6:27 _____

_____

John 7:37–38 _____

_____

Acts 1:8 _____

_____

39 LET THE STREAMS FLOW
STARTING TO SWIM

Write out your *testi*mony in point-form below. Record what your testing was and how it hurt—how God helped you and was water to you in your desert time—how God saved you, not how you got out of the desert by yourself! Record your victory and hope for the future. If it's a current struggle God is helping you through, write that down, and make sure you write hope for the future.

Share your testimony with someone in the next week. Come back and record what happens.

Romans 8:28, 31–37

_____

_____

_____

_____

_____

1 Corinthians 15:57–58

_____

_____

_____

_____

_____

John 16:20

_____

_____

_____

_____

_____

John 16:33

_____

_____

_____

_____

_____

Isaiah 49:10

Isaiah 55:1

Psalm 27:13

Psalm 71:20–21

No More Tears
40 Starting to Swim

Take a look at the eight promises in Revelation that are addressed to those who overcome. May your ear be open to hear the encouragement of the Spirit telling you that you're an overcomer. Write down the promises in each passage.

- When you come across it, highlight the words *"He who has an ear, let him hear what the Spirit says to the churches."*
- In another color, highlight the words *"To him/ He/Him who overcomes."* Underline the promise that is given to overcomers.

Revelations 2:7 _____

_____

_____

_____

Revelation 2:11 _____

_____

_____

_____

Revelation 2:17 (Also read John 6:48–63. The key verses are 6:48–51, 63.) _____

_____

_____

_____

Revelation 2:26–27 _____

    Who will Jesus give authority to? _____

_____

_____

Where did Jesus' authority come from? _____

_____

_____

Revelation 3:5–6 _____

_____

_____

Revelation 3:12–13 _____

_____

_____

Revelation 3:21–22 _____

_____

_____

Compare this verse to Revelation 7:17. _____

_____

_____

Revelation 21:7 _____

_____

_____

_____

ABOUT THE AUTHOR

Todd and Sherry Stahl

Some might say that the author was named prophetically. Born to John and Sharon Fletcher of Hamilton, Ontario, Canada, she was named Sherry Lynn Fletcher. The name Lynn is of Gaelic origin and refers to a lake, waterfall, pool, or person living near a body of water. In her early thirties, Sherry received a bookmark from one of the girls who attended a Bible study she taught. It had her middle name on it, with a definition of the name. The bookmark read "Lynn... one who refreshes others." It is her prayer that through this book, God has used her to be one who truly does refresh others.

Sherry has felt the call of God on her life to make a difference in this world since she was nine years old, and more directly when she was nineteen. She is a Bible college graduate and was a youth pastor in her twenties. Sherry has two wonderful children, Brandon and Shelby. For years, she has been involved in ministry to women through teaching Bible studies as well as speaking at women's groups and retreats. For over ten years, she was the director of finance and operations for a very successful business in the automotive industry. Her hobbies range from scrapbooking to drag racing!

The Sahara of Sherry's desert time took place during her marital breakdown, and more acutely when her daughter was struggling with clinical depression. Out of these desert times, God gave her water, like He did Hagar, which inspired the book. When her daughter's depression hit its lowest level and medication changes caused extreme mood instability, Sherry felt that she, too, was slipping into depression. While lying on the couch one morning, ready to give in to hopelessness, she felt God challenging her to trust Shelby with Him. He also challenged her that if she truly was going to trust Him, she would begin to move forward into the call He had placed on her to write. She chose to trust, and began to write. The fruit of this obedience is held in your hands, and in the health that her daughter has begun to walk in.

In the goodness of God, He brought a wonderful man into Sherry's life. Todd Stahl is not only the illustrator of this book, but a wonderful second chance at true love. He is the man Sherry dreamed of as a teenager—a partner in life, love, friendship, and ministry! Creating this book together has been a dream realized! They are finishing their next book together, *Turn Scars into Stars*, which will display one of Todd's paintings. This will be another dream fulfilled, for both of them! Sherry looks forward to the future, where God's plans keep unfolding!

To learn more about Sherry, her blog, other writings, and her speaking engagements, you can connect with her:

Website: www.sherrystahl.com
Blog: www.soul-h2o.com
Email: info@sherrystahl.com

Linked in   Sherry Stahl

twitter   sherry_stahl

Instagram   sherry_stahl

facebook.   Water in the Desert Book

Sherry Stahl
Christian Author & Speaker

Sherry is a dynamic Bible study, retreat, event, and conference speaker. She loves to passionately share with people the message of God's goodness to bring them water in their desert! Sherry enjoys connecting with women of all ages and loves when she has the opportunity to speak into the lives of teen girls with her {PURE} beauty retreats! Invite Sherry to speak at your event!

To book Sherry for an event,
email: booking@sherrystahl.com
www.sherrystahl.com

Looking for some inspiration?

Check out Sherry's blog at

www.soul-h2o.com

Weekly devotionals are posted every Monday.

You can read posts in four categories
that will leave your soul refreshed!

Devotionals   Real Life
Ministry Life   Interesting Stuff

BRINGING WATER TO PEOPLE WHO NEED IT

At least ten percent of proceeds from this book will be given to ministries who bring clean water to people in need. Partner with Sherry and these ministries to create a greater impact!

 ## STREAMS IN THE DESERT PROJECT

Digging 12 large-volume, solar-powered wells to provide a constant source of clean water for 1275 Families! Each Family will have a 1/4 acre property to farm, enabling them to provide food year round for themselves since they will be drought-proof! As Section six in the book teaches, God provides Water that Grows Gardens!

He makes our "deserts like Eden...wastelands like the garden of the Lord." Isaiah 51:3 (NIV)

WWW.CROSSROADS.CA/RELIEF-DEVELOPMENT

ABOUT THE ILLUSTRATOR

After attending college for graphic design, Todd was involved in a family-run business for twenty years, but the search was always on to do something more related to his gifting. Taking steps towards pursuing his dreams, Todd became a firefighter in 2004 and is now certified across North America. Moving closer to the heart of his dreams, Todd has rekindled his passion for art. His desire is to continue creating thought-provoking pieces of art. Working alongside his wife Sherry, providing the art and often inspiration for *Water in the Desert* was enjoyable and rewarding. Being a part of the process inspired Todd to write his own book! Todd has published a men's devotional called *40 Days in the Man Cave*—a book for the manly man in your life!

To view more of Todd's work and upcoming projects, please visit his website.

www.toddstahl.com
info@toddstahl.com

Know someone else who should try The 40 Day Challenge? Meet the men's counterpart to *Water in the Desert: 40 Days in the Man Cave* by Todd Stahl!

> *"A man needs another man to talk to him about the deep stuff...Todd Stahl is that man, and 40 Days in the Man Cave is that straight talk. It's clear, fair, honest, and true. Have a listen yourself."*
>
> —Mark Buchanan
> Author of Your Church is Too Safe

Guys, we all know life is crazy busy. We can be inundated with tasks, jobs, commitments, and activities. The truth is, men need to find a place to get away, chill out, and reenergize. Wherever your man cave may be, carve out a few minutes each day to refuel in it.

You are Water in My Desert

Rachelle Fletcher is a singer-songwriter who has recorded two albums. She has lead worship in the Dallas-Fort Worth area in Texas for more than 22 years. With a passion for spreading the Gospel and a heart for saving unborn babies, Rachelle uses her vast business experience to serve as the Executive Director of Real Choices in Grapevine. Rachelle lives in the Fort Worth, area with her husband of 24 years and two beautiful daughters, Brianna and Katelynn.

Her song, *You are Water in My Desert*, was inspired by Sherry's own desert journey. Sherry and Rachelle hope this song will encourage you on your journey as well.

Please log on to
www.rachellefletcher.com
to hear a recording of the song.